ALSO BY DOROTHY GALLAGHER

*How I Came into My Inheritance
and Other True Stories*

*All the Right Enemies: The Life and
Murder of Carlo Tresca*

*Hannah's Daughters: Six Generations of
an American Family, 1876–1976*

Strangers in the House

Strangers in the House

Life Stories

Dorothy Gallagher

RANDOM HOUSE · NEW YORK

Published in the United States by Random
House, an imprint of The Random House
Publishing Group, a division of Random
House, Inc., New York.

RANDOM HOUSE and colophon are registered
trademarks of Random House, Inc.

"Whoever You Were" was previously
published in *Epoch*, volume 53, number 2
(2004). "Mystery Woman Ruled Dead;
Lost Since Break with Reds" was previously
published in a different form as
"Disappeared" in *Grand Street*, volume 9,
number 2 (Winter 1990). "Jury Duty" was
previously published in a different form as
"A Murder in Morningside Park" in *The New
York Times Magazine* (August 28, 1977).
"Strangers in the House" was previously
published in *More* (March 2006).

Grateful acknowledgment is made to
Harcourt, Inc. for permission to reprint an
excerpt from "List" and an excerpt from
"Among the Multitudes" from *Monologue
of a Dog* by Wislawa Szymborska, copyright
© 2002 by Wislawa Szymborska, English
translation copyright © 2006 by Harcourt, Inc.
Reprinted by permission of Harcourt, Inc.

Photo credits can be found on page 145.

Library of Congress Cataloging-in-Publication
Data

Gallagher, Dorothy.
Strangers in the house:
life stories / Dorothy Gallagher.
p.   cm.
Contents: The making of me—Whoever you
were—What you see is what you get—
Mystery woman ruled dead—Jury duty—In
the vicinity of art—Foucault's last lover—
Stay—Strangers in the house—Dumb luck.
ISBN 1-4000-6257-8
1. Gallagher, Dorothy.   2. New York
(N.Y.)—Biography.   I. Title.

CT275.G248A3 2006
974.7'1043'092—dc22   2005051650

Printed in the United States of America
on acid-free paper

www.atrandom.com

9 8 7 6 5 4 3 2 1

First Edition

Book design by David Goldstein

To Ben

I've made a list of questions
to which I no longer expect answers,
since it's either too early for them,
or I won't have time to understand.

—WISLAWA SZYMBORSKA

Contents

Strangers in the House

The Making of Me

I ran into Jack Hoffman on the street. I hadn't seen him in ages.

We said "How are you?" and "What's new?"

"Did you hear?" he said. "Victor's dead. Heart attack. Five years ago."

"Really?" I said.

"Yes," he said. "Really."

"Dr. Nielsen?" I said the first time I went to his office.

He nodded. He never argued with that form of address.

This was Victor Nielsen, not any sort of doctor; a former opera singer (Danish). Those were the days when anyone could hang out a shingle as a "lay" analyst.

You might expect a Dane to be tall and blond. Not so Victor. He was about fifty then, not in the least handsome, short and stocky, with a fleshy face. But he had a large head, thick gray hair, and he looked bigger sitting down. Sitting down was a major part of his job. Also he had very blue eyes; and his low, well-trained, charmingly accented voice, a beautiful voice, which gave him great authority; and in the end you had to say that, all in all, he was an attractive man.

His office was somewhere on the Upper West Side, Eighty-sixth Street, I think, just a few doors in from Broadway. It was a large room, bright, uncurtained, just above street level. Standing, you had a perfect view of the street life below; sitting, you saw the heads of people walking past the windows. I sat across the desk from Victor. ("Call me Victor," he said, waving away any need for the spurious title.) I had expected a leather couch, but his office contained only the desk, a couple of chairs, a Marimekko sort of rug, and a daybed with a rough cotton throw, drab blue, as I remember. In due course, I thought, I would be invited to lie down.

Why was I there? Hindsight shows me that I was just ahead of the sea change. Only a few years later, a nineteen-year-old girl—confused, moody, depressed, reluctantly promiscuous—would be engulfed by a culture and a cause—drugs, casual sex, communes, Vietnam; would know what clothes to wear—vintage dresses, army castoffs, jeans, T-shirts; would know how to do her hair—parted in the middle, flowing down her back; and would know what music belonged to her—Dylan, Baez, etc. As it was, I wore the hateful garter belts and stockings of my time, straight woolen skirts and shirtwaist dresses; set my hair every night to appear as a shoulder-length pageboy in the morning; listened to Frank Sinatra and Vaughn Monroe, who certainly weren't bad but weren't mine.

My mother was at her wits' end. She consulted her cousin Sylvia, the social worker.

"I can't deal with her," my mother said. "She leaves school, she stays out all night, she won't tell me where she goes, she moves out of the house, she moves back in, she can't keep a job, she won't talk to me."

Sylvia, being a social worker, knew what to do. "Send her to an analyst," she said. "I know someone."

So now I was sitting across the desk from my analyst, and what did he say to me?

"I'm going to make a real little woman out of you."

Once a week, over a couple of years, I saw Victor Nielsen. Apart from that promise, which he often repeated, I can't remember another word of what passed between us. No doubt I talked about my mother, my father, and how they had ruined my life. At the time, I happened to be lovesick for a man who would marry me two years later; in the meantime, he had dumped me, and I was sleeping with almost anyone who asked. Each time I told Victor about one of these incidents, he said, "You have the makings of a real little woman."

Who was right about this: Victor? Or my father, who had taken to calling me a prostitute?

Well of course I was not a prostitute, although I could see where he might get that idea. If he had known about it, for instance, my father could have said that I once did it for a dime. I was visiting San Francisco, and a guy whose name I no longer remember had kindly taken me to see the sights. We spent a long day together, and then a long evening. After dinner he suggested we spend the night together. I was staying across the Bay, in Berkeley, with my cousin Vivian. It was late, it was raining, I was tired. I didn't particularly like this guy, and furthermore, I had my period. I thought about this. And then I thought about waiting for the bus, which ran infrequently at that hour, about the long bus ride to Berkeley, and about the walk through the rain to my cousin's house. The dime was the bus fare.

I had once briefly shared an apartment with a girl who was desperate to lose her virginity. She was very strange. The things that happened to me happened to girls all the time. And it was always easier to say yes. "No" was impolite. "No" would be taken personally.

"Why not?" the guy would say incredulously. "Don't you like me?" That was a possibility so far out of the question, it had never entered his mind.

Or he might get mean: "Are you frigid?"

Such a foolish girl! So acquiescent to the imperious male. So careful of his pride. One night I let such a guy, prideful, imperious, take me to bed. He was not only married, he was impotent, and he wanted to keep trying again and again. It was extremely unpleasant. Finally, I said, "No, really, no more." I was very nice. I didn't mention that I was sore and exhausted and repelled. I didn't mention that he didn't have the wherewithal. I politely said, "Listen, I know you're married; I don't like one-night stands."

He turned vicious. "You better get used to one-night stands," he said, "because that's all you're ever going to have."

You'd think that Victor might have helped me out with these situations.

After a couple of years, Bob and I got married, and I didn't see Victor again until Bob and I separated three years later. By that time I had a boyfriend named Jack. (Yes, that Jack; the Jack who would tell me that Victor had died.) And here's where the story gets interesting.

Jack had once been married to a girl named Sheila. Sheila was not happy in the marriage. She went to see an analyst. Guess who? Victor! And guess who Sheila was now married to? Victor! They had a little baby.

"Really?" I said.

By the way, I said to Victor, "Isn't this situation—you, me, Jack, Sheila, all of us involved in one way and another—isn't it, well, a problem for you, professionally speaking?"

"No problem," Victor said. "You'll like Sheila. She was a confused little girl when she first came to see me, but now she's a real little woman." He added, "You and Jack, you come and spend a weekend with us."

Jack and I spent several weekends with Victor and Sheila. We all became good friends. Of course, I saw more of Victor than that, since he was still my analyst.

One day I told Victor I was tired of Jack.

"Ah," Victor said.

And it seemed that due course had arrived.

Victor took my hand and led me to the daybed with the blue cotton cover. I lay down. In that position I could no longer see people walking by on the street. All I could see was Victor's fleshy face looming over me. He murmured in my ear: "You see? You're a real little woman now."

Whoever You Were

I was living up on Ninety-ninth and Broadway, remember? In that studio on the fifteenth floor? Only one window, the kitchen hidden in a closet like a Murphy bed. I liked that apartment. No surprises, no one lurking in another room.

Sure, you remember that place. You lurked across the street most of that cold winter, sometimes late into the night, watching the entrance, waiting to catch the man I preferred to you.

How in God's name did you think you'd ever spot him, anyway? Do you know how many apartments there were in that building? Sixty, seventy apartments, maybe. Men coming and going all the time. Men who lived in that building, one of whom, I'll tell you now, was my lover. Jack. Jack, who lived one flight above me. It was a joke.

No, no, not a joke. I only made jokes because I was appalled. What had I done? And Bob, dear Bob, sweet Bob, you were out of control, you were over the edge. Crazy Bob. Remember the

New Year's Eve after I left? You rang my doorbell. Jack was with me. I was afraid to let you in, I was afraid not to. I said, "This is Jack, my upstairs neighbor." At last you had caught me with a man, and you didn't put two and two together. Why not? Of course, Jack was just this really short guy, not attractive, not even to me, but still, you must have wanted not to know. If you'd known, you'd have had to hit him with those brass knuckles you were carrying around. Brass knuckles! Where the hell did you get brass knuckles?

Jack left, and then we were alone. I asked you to leave too, but you wouldn't. You were acting so nice and friendly, smiling, it was all wrong, you scared me, Bob. I went into the bathroom and locked the door. I stayed there until you finally gave up and I heard the door close behind you. Only later did I realize you'd gotten what you came for. You found my address book. You wrote down the telephone number of every man listed (there were only three or four possible candidates, weren't there? The others were my therapist, my cousins, our friends), and you called each of them. Somehow you got a couple of them to agree to meet you, and you bought them a drink. They told me you had smiled at them in what you thought was the friendliest way, and you demanded that each one admit he was the guy. They denied it. Who wouldn't deny it, you with your menacing smile and your right pocket bulging with brass knuckles? And then you went to see my therapist, and he told my mother, and then she started sending me clippings from the *Daily Mirror*: HUSBAND KILLS ESTRANGED WIFE! HUSBAND KILLS LOVER OF ESTRANGED WIFE, ESTRANGED WIFE AND SELF!

What had I done? I wasn't used to being so effective. And I have to say, it was very exciting, the drama of it all.

• • •

Remember Beth Kelly? Wasn't she beautiful? So blond and delicate. Oh my God, so many years have passed I wouldn't know her if she sat down next to me. (Would I know you now? Or you me, as far as that goes?) Beth wanted to be a movie star, she could have been a movie star, but I guess she never made it. If not for Beth, I might never have left you.

When Beth came home from summer stock that fall, she was pregnant. You knew that, didn't you? Two months pregnant. It could have been Larry's baby: he'd gone to visit her once or twice that summer. She could have said it was Larry's.

We were all living in the West Village then, practically in the same house; you and I separated by one brownstone wall from Larry and Beth. I can see those houses as clearly as if we still lived there. I still marvel at the rent—the whole house, four floors, for $250, heat included. I remember all the places we lived and how we furnished them. I remember that awful black platform couch we bought at the Door Store, and the crewel wing chair I bought secondhand from an ad in *The Village Voice*. (It was $25, and I felt so smug because Harold and Joan had paid $350 at Macy's for one exactly like it.)

The day after Beth got home, she came over to see me. It was in early September, such a hot day. I was in the kitchen with the door to the backyard wide open. I was glad to see her; I'd missed her. She looked a little pale, though, and I said something like, Gee, Beth, you look tired, are you okay? And she said, No, I'm pregnant. I said, Really! She just looked at me. So then I said, Do you want it? And she said, No. It's not Larry's. I'm not having it. I'm getting a divorce.

Adultery. Abortion. Divorce. I can't tell you how that constellation hit me. Honestly, I think I only knew those words from novels. Beth and Larry were our friends, they'd gotten married a few weeks before we did, they had dinner with us almost every other night, they went to the movies with us, we sat talking at Pete's Tavern for hours. We were a foursome. If those huge words had to do with them, what about us? What about me? Was I allowed? Not that I had committed Adultery. Not yet. Not that I was Pregnant. Not yet.

We weren't doing well, you knew that. Two years into marriage, and sex was such a sometime thing. That was my doing. Remember the time you'd been away in Chicago for a week? When you came home, I didn't want to. And you said, "You know, I had plenty of chances in Chicago, but I wanted you."

Yes. I knew how attractive you could be to women. Hadn't I been one of them myself? It seemed like only yesterday I had wanted you, and all the time; I'd been desperate to marry you for three years, miserable while you went out with this one and that one—Della, Phyllis, Alice, Ruth . . . And then you capitulated. Entirely, with your whole heart you gave yourself to me, I became the one who was halfhearted. So I had what I had wanted, and I was unhappy all the time.

I'm remembering something else: a few weeks after you got home from Chicago, we went out to dinner at one of those French restaurants on Fifty-fifth or Fifty-sixth Street; Steak Frites, I think it was, there used to be so many of those cheap and decent little French restaurants then. Did we sit silently over our meal? Did we speak cold monosyllables? At one point you got up from the table, maybe you went to the bathroom or to make a phone call. The owner of the café came over to me. She said, "Did you know the gentleman sitting alone at that table?" She pointed. I turned. The table behind us was empty. I said, "No, I didn't notice him." She handed me an envelope. She said, "The gentleman was by himself, he said it was his birthday, and he wanted you to have this." There was nothing written on the envelope, there was no note inside, only a ten-dollar bill. Ten dollars wasn't a lot of money even in those days. And this is what I imagined: the man, middle-aged (he was probably younger than we are today), had watched us at our silent dinner. What did he see? A thin young girl with short dark hair, silent, sad; a redheaded man, a little older, frustrated and angry because the girl was so sullen. The observing man wanted to tell the girl something. That she was pretty? That she reminded him of someone in his past? That things would get better for her, maybe? The French restaurant, the young unhappy couple, the older man eating his lonely birthday dinner in a cheap restaurant, telling himself our story. Romantic, wasn't it?

Joan. Now, Joan was happy. She was pregnant and happy, she and Harold were happy. I said, "Joan, I'm so unhappy, what should I do?" She said, "Stop nagging him. Bob's great. Maybe he's a little erratic, but that's the way he is. He's brilliant."

Yes, it's true: you were erratic, brilliant, flying one minute, crashing the next, full of grandiose plans I didn't understand, drinking too much, eating too much. And then somebody would put a spoke in your wheel at work, or I'd say, "Bob, you're crazy, you can't just build a hydrogen balloon . . . whatever!"

You know, the strange thing is that I can hear you, your beautiful lilting tenor, singing one of those corny Irish ballads you used to sing to me . . . *"She was lovely and fair as the first* rose of summer / *But it was not her beauty alone that won me* / *Oh no, t'was the truth in her eyes ever shining* / *That made me love Mary, the Rose of Tralee* . . ." But I can't bring back the sound of your voice when you spoke to me.

No, I wouldn't go with you in any hydrogen balloon, but I did something just as dangerous. I went on the *Athlone* with you. I remember so many things about that boat: it was twenty-three feet long, it had a steel hull, it had been built in Holland, it was a sloop—a mainsail, a jib, ropes that rubbed my fingers raw, a minuscule cabin with two bunks, each wide enough to sleep a snake. I got on board and let you sail me from Gravesend Bay, up the East River, and all the way to Martha's Vineyard, with no motor except a three-horsepower outboard that conked out in the Narrows.

You didn't know a thing about sailing, did you, except what you taught yourself from a book. That's where you were so brilliant. You could teach yourself anything, the most complicated technical things, from a book. Remember when you told me that boats under sail always have the right of way? If you knew so much, why did we nearly drown when that cruise ship didn't change course in New York Harbor?

Three long weeks on the tiny boat, sometimes heeled so far over that the mainsail skimmed the water; tacking back and forth, back and forth across the Sound; becalmed in fog for a day and night; on a roller coaster of stormy seas; soaking-wet bunks; eating canned corned beef hash morning, noon, and night. (Oh, sometimes Dinty Moore beef stew.) I wanted to scream! But we had some moments, didn't we? Like that perfect evening, the time of day when the wind dies and the sea goes flat. We were tied up in a harbor, down in the cabin heating up hash over the Sterno stove, when there was a bump against the boat. We climbed up on deck. A school of porpoises was circling the boat, playing with it, playing with us, jumping out of the water, bumping us, circling round and round. They stayed with us for almost an hour as the sun went down, they were close enough to touch, and I did, I reached down and petted one as he swam by. He seemed to jump for joy. That was a glory, wasn't it?

And that sun-struck day in open ocean, out of sight of land, zipping right along on a following wind. On impulse I took off my clothes, jumped into the water . . . and surfaced all alone in the middle of the ocean, the *Athlone* sailing on until it was just a speck, almost to the horizon. It took such a long, long time for you to head into the wind, turn the boat around, tack, tack, tack back for me, but you did it, I knew you could, I treaded water and waited for you.

It was Helen who brought me to 85 Perry Street that first night. Maybe you don't remember Helen—my friend from Hunter, Jerry's girlfriend for a little while. She passed through Perry Street pretty quickly, she passed through my life pretty quickly too. But she brought me to that house, and what a house it was, two floors of it, wide-plank floorboards, and four older guys (in your late twenties to our eighteen, a lifetime older) living in what seemed like a perpetual party, girlfriends coming and going—a wonder of a place to a girl from Washington Heights, how I wanted to be one of those girlfriends.

I was brought for you that night. But oh no; at the last minute Della had to push her way in. "A party!" said Della. "Can I come?" Helen looked at me. I said okay. What else could I say? I would have said no if Della hadn't been so pretty; I had my pride. You remember Della: tall, blond, a knockout. You took her home that night.

Oh, that was a cruel blow! Because I had already planned my life around you. Yes, the minute I saw you, I knew that you would mean the world to me. Just that. The world. My Open Sesame.

Della wouldn't last long. You were too rough a diamond for Della, she thought too well of herself, she thought she was entitled to more polish, better social credentials. But for me, you were more than good enough, whoever you were.

I wrote to you last year. Did you get my letter? Did you not remember who I was? Or did you just decide you didn't want to answer? Were you too medicated to answer? Yes, I know you're medicated, that you've been in the hospital. Depression, Harold told me; he says you talk very slowly. That must be the medication. Do you know that Joan died?

Harold is the only one I still know from our time together. Helen, Beth, Della—they all disappeared from my life. I wanted to tell you that I remember everything that happened to us. All the big things—love, marriage, abortion, adultery, divorce—happened to us, happened first to us. I know that you married again, that you have two children, grown now, that you sit quietly all day with a book on your lap, reading, or maybe just staring at the page.

Another thing I wanted to mention. About the cold winter when you still lived on Perry Street, and you were going out with Ruth, Alice, Della, Phyllis, whoever. And I was crazy with love for you and lurked across from your house late into the night, waiting to see you with the girl you preferred to me.

What You See Is What You Get

By 1970 I had lived in Brooklyn Heights for five or six years, and during the last couple of years I was on my own. Every morning I rode the subway under the river to my job at a magazine in the city; every evening I came back to that peaceful, leafy enclave. So peaceful. So leafy.

Sometimes, for a change of scene, I'd walk the length of the Promenade to the north end, and down the steep hill that led to the gritty flats on the river. If not for some ancient faces peering from tenement windows—relics of the once-thriving waterfront—you would have thought that the streets under the Brooklyn Bridge were deserted. The buildings fronting the river looked like a movie set waiting for action. Among the boarded-up shops was one café still in business, although it was empty the day I happened to take a picture of it.

I look at that photograph now, and it takes me back to a lonely time: my twenties were recent history, my marriage was behind me, my Nikon was in my hand, and I was searching for a way into the picture. I'm reminded that the day was windy, the air was fresh, a hard bright light glanced off the choppy river. And here is the picture I took: a plate-glass window with RESTAURANT in gilt, half chipped off. On the far side of the window, you can see the café in wait: metal-ringed Formica tables set with napkin holders, glass sugar dispensers, and salt and pepper shakers, their metal tops gleaming in the sun. And there, in the reflection of the window, is my shadow, the light-struck river, and the Manhattan skyline behind, like a city dreamed of. A block or two away, out of camera range, is the house where Norman Peterson lived.

Norman Peterson had found a dilapidated two-room building to hold his precarious life. Upstairs he slept on a cot and made his strange metal sculptures; the dark downstairs room was the kitchen. When you got to know him, you felt that those rooms, in the deep shadow of the soaring span of the bridge, enveloped by the constant hum of interborough traffic, smelling of the gas station next door, were his natural home.

Norman came from Seattle. His uncle was a commercial fisherman. As a boy, Norman had worked the boats. He talked sometimes about winter expeditions up Puget Sound and on to the coast of Alaska, the temperature so low that salt spray froze his eyes shut. He got away from that life by joining the army. After that, on the GI Bill, he took a course in welding, thinking it would be a useful trade to keep him on land. Then something unsuspected happened. He began to make sculptures from the metal he welded. He was an artist! He knew it! And where in the world did that ever come from, a boy who'd never known an artist, seen an art book, much less been to a museum? A boy from as deep into the working class as you could get.

And then he really got out. He went to live the artist's life on an Aegean island—Hydra—where a colony of artists had migrated. He told me who they were, but the only one I remember is Leonard Cohen. It was a paradise: sunshine every day, work in the morning, swimming in the afternoon, dinners that went on into the small hours, Leonard Cohen singing his songs, vast quantities of vile wine and willing women.

Hydra was Norman's moment: he'd found his way into a life. But then Leonard Cohen left the island ("So long, Marianne . . ."), and the colony disintegrated. Where else do artists congregate? Norman came to my cold, costly city, where no gallery was interested in his work and the circles of artists were closed to him. He went on working, but no one saw his work, and certainly no one bought his work. He found an old panel truck and made a living as a moving man.

When I met Norman, he was in his late thirties, though you might easily have guessed forties. He had a truck driver's build: big and lumbering, strong, with a beer belly. He rolled his own cigarettes. He usually wore a hat, a Greek fisherman's cap in winter, a straw hat tilted against the sun in summer. I liked his looks—his height, his physical strength, his black hair and mustache, his clear gray eyes. But I was put off too: he was wary, mostly silent, gruff when he spoke. Conversation was definitely not his sport.

I was of two minds about Norman. Sometimes I thought of him as an innocent fool, without vanity or self-consciousness, without a clue as to how much of a misfit he was. His social skills were close to nil, which carried over to the arts of flirtation and flattery. He had no idea how to make use of himself with women—with urban women, anyway; uptown girls, he called them, girls like me. (I suspect he was accustomed to more direct transactions with women.) But I had other moods when I saw him as the gold standard, a simon-pure original, aware of it, and on guard against assaults to his integrity.

In practical terms, of course, the distinction didn't matter. He was, he always would be, elusive, isolated, an oddball. Yes, I was interested, but I knew that what I saw was what I'd get. I never lost my heart. So when the lease on my apartment ran out and Norman said, "Live with me," I laughed. That was mean. But really, did he think my prospects were so dim that I would make my life with a de facto hermit in his dank dark hovel?

Now Wendy Samson, she had a way with her.

"Oh hi! I'm so glad to meet you!" she would say on meeting someone new. "I loved your piece about . . ." and Wendy would turn to a person nearby and tell that person that you were a brilliant writer, painter, poet . . . whatever it was you happened to profess. Then she would inform you that this other person was also brilliant at something or other. Simply being introduced to Wendy Samson brought membership in a coterie of brilliant people, who seemed to be the only sort of people Wendy knew. I was quite taken with her.

Wendy and I had recently become colleagues. We were staff writers at a famous magazine for young women, which meant that we got a salary for which we owed the magazine a certain number of articles a year. We didn't have to go into the office very often, and we could also write for other publications. It was a terrific job. A sort of subsidized freelance career.

I wasn't able to match Wendy's flattery, as I hadn't yet read anything she'd written. But I'd heard her spoken of in admiring terms as a rising star of journalism (celebrity profiles, reports from the cultural front). Wendy had the looks for media stardom. She was about thirty then, tall, leggy, slender, a little stooped, as tall girls often were in those days. But her thick black hair cascaded down her back. She wore aviator glasses in the style made ubiquitous—required, even—by Gloria Steinem, who was her hero (role model, as we used to say) and who also happened to wear her hair the same way. And, as pretty young women with good legs did, as Gloria Steinem did, Wendy dressed in miniskirts. She was filled with nervous energy: her foot jiggled, she leaned in close, her speech was rushed, confiding, avid.

Although I hadn't read Wendy's pieces, I had read about her in an interview in which Wendy and her husband conversed on the subject of the "two-career marriage." Her husband was, naturally, a brilliant academic; Wendy, brilliant in her own way, had chosen a career in the popular prints. She and her husband, by compromising when necessary, by giving each other the gift of loving respect and maneuvering room, had made their marriage into a triumphant model of modern relations between the sexes. A photograph accompanied the article: beautiful Wendy holding hands with her very handsome husband. They were an enviable couple. So when I mentioned to Wendy that I was looking for an apartment and she suggested that I share hers, well, you can imagine my surprise.

The husband had fled. Another woman. Wendy was shocked, devastated, brave. I went to inspect the former marital home. It was one of those vast, rambling apartments on the

Upper West Side. There was a huge foyer, a large living room, a dining room, a bedroom wing with two bedrooms, each with a bath, and somewhere in the dim recesses, a maid's room and a kitchen. The main rooms were heavily furnished with vaguely Spanish-style furniture, large pieces that seemed not so much chosen as too much trouble to remove.

I looked around. The apartment could be split down the middle: a bedroom for me, the dining room turned into my living room; we'd share the kitchen. I had a few reservations. I was used to living on my own, and for the most part, I liked it. I didn't have such a good history of living with people—roommates in the distant past, husbands more recently. But I knew something about solitude: it could easily become too much of a good thing.

"Yes, okay," I said to Wendy. "Let's try it."

Norman helped me pack my belongings into his panel truck. He moved me in late one night and stayed until morning. For Norman, Wendy varied her formula: "Oh, he's so interesting, isn't he?" she said.

I didn't see as much of Norman Peterson after that. He came uptown from time to time, usually unannounced. One evening he brought me a sculpture. It looked like a heart—a real heart, I mean, an anatomical heart, with the aorta attached—or maybe like a heavy-bottomed seabird with a narrow head. He said he was starting to do ceramics again, and that he was thinking about making lamps.

"Sell them to those designers," he said. "Make some money."

"Good idea," I said.

"How are you doing?" he asked. "Like living here?"

Did I like living there?

By then I'd been living at Wendy's for about six months, and it was beginning to seem like the central fact of my life. In theory we shared the apartment: we split the rent, we each had a set of rooms, separate lives. Yes, I could close my door, do my work, see friends. But by some alchemy, Wendy filled all the space. I never knew quite how she did it. She was like a black hole: all matter, all energy that entered her gravitational field, was sucked in. Late at night (she stayed up very late), late in the morning (she got up very late), I heard her shuffling footsteps going past my closed door. I felt reproach in her every step. Because what was I doing when my door was closed?

I wasn't helping Wendy!

Wendy was afflicted. Naturally. Her husband had chosen another. Actually, it was something more material than Wendy's negative energy that took up so much room. Many days and many nights, three or four of her friends were summoned to console her. Occasionally, her daytime phone invitations—"Do you want to go for a walk in the park?"—or the late-evening calls— "Come over and let's talk"—failed to produce anybody, and Wendy found herself alone. How she hated being alone! When that happened, she came to my room, her bathrobe scruffy, her hair lank, advertising depression. She sat on the edge of my bed and talked and talked. She rehearsed the years of her marriage, the unforgivable betrayal that she had done nothing to deserve (indeed, she had been the most generous and loving of wives). I listened. At first I was sympathetic. I'd been there.

But with each retelling of the story, a little more information slipped out. Perhaps Wendy hadn't been such a loving wife after all. Perhaps, she said (with what I would call a snicker), she had become bored with marital sex and had had a few affairs with the celebrity subjects of her interviews.

"Well. But Wendy. If you were having sex with everybody except your husband . . ."

Wendy was affronted: "But he didn't know that," she wailed.

How could I be so insensitive?

And did I say that three or four of Wendy's friends would appear almost daily? Seven or eight of her friends. Old school friends, strangers passing through town who'd gotten Wendy's name from some acquaintance, it made no matter. They slept in the maid's room, they slept on the couches, they stayed for days, sometimes weeks. And what did they do in her apartment, in my apartment? They helped Wendy.

All night long—because Wendy liked nothing more than to be awake in the small hours, talking about her crisis—they consoled her, they gossiped with her, some slept with her. And, being brilliant, each and every one, they helped her write her pieces. They went over her notes, they helped her organize them, they showed her where the narrative was, they found her lead, they worked out the sentences. Now that just drove me up the wall.

Did I like living there?

I went to Brooklyn to see Norman's lamps. I was astonished. I was used to his weird, abstract, distinctly unbeautiful pieces. These were gorgeous. Steel, glowing like old pewter, made sweeping arcs through the air. They were more than sculptural, they were sculptures. Beautiful.

"They're beautiful," I said. "Anybody would want them. I want one. There's one problem."

"What?"

"It's not a lamp if there's hardly any light."

Norman considered. Would a lamp that actually illuminated ruin his artistic intent?

"I don't know," he said.

He was so annoying. Didn't he want to sell them? Didn't he want some worldly reward?

Norman and I were not lovers anymore, but he kept in touch. He kept in touch more than I liked. He hoped. Had the words been available to him, I think he would have said he loved me. At any rate, he aspired to me.

I was seriously thinking about moving. It was such a drag to move. Looking for another place, packing up everything, unpacking, organizing stuff, my work interrupted for weeks. But you can imagine: my life was a nightmare. Even if you don't want to go to the party, you want to be asked to the party. I knew that I had brought it all on myself. My disdain for Wendy's life—what would in later years be called her "lifestyle"—was palpable.

Many nights I felt imprisoned in my room. I was reluctant even to walk through the crowd to go to the kitchen. One night, outside my door, the Hog Farm had gathered. Remember the Hog Farm? I had not bargained for this, for life in a dorm, life at summer camp. And just as there is a pariah at every summer camp, I was the outcast here, the wet blanket, the sourpuss, the person consumed with envy—at Wendy's success: her social and professional success (yes, many famous men, all of them brilliant, naturally, sought her out to sexually console her; once consolation had taken place, they were pressed into helping Wendy with her work—into doing her work). Well, no, I never had asked anyone for help, but why was no one offering to console me? To help me? Oh, and did I mention that Wendy's brother was now living in the apartment full-time, another tenant without a by-your-leave? Golly, I was bitter.

I took a week off and went to Monhegan Island, where my friend Kitty was staying. I must have mentioned it to Norman, because the day after I got to the island, I ran into him toiling up the hill from the ferry, wearing his straw summer hat tilted against the sun. He was in good spirits. People had liked his lamps. Galleries were dubious, but a high-end shop had taken a few on consignment. "Yeah," he said, "I made the light brighter."

He asked me where I was staying. "Do you have your own room?"

I had my own room at the hotel. Yes, he could stay with me. It was summer, I was on vacation, he had come all this way for me. Why not? "But Norman," I said, "this doesn't change anything." Norman's lovemaking had never been persuasive enough to change anything.

When I got back to the city, I told Wendy that I'd be moving out as soon as I found a place.

"Not until October," she said. "I need to find another roommate."

"You have another roommate," I said. "Your brother lives

here. And, from night to night, so do any number of other people. Rosemary, Derek, Peter, Mary, the Hog Farm . . . I could go on."

"You know," she said, "your friend Kitty stayed here one night, and you didn't even ask me."

She had me there.

I found a place at the end of July. A loft downtown, on the Bowery. I packed my clothes, my papers, my books. Everything was in cartons. I came home one afternoon to find Wendy's brother unpacking my book cartons.

"What are you doing?"

"Wendy says you took her *New York Times Cookbook*."

"It's my *New York Times Cookbook*," I said. And how dare you?

A food fight. Exactly the right parting note.

I got out of there. I felt so light I was floating, dancing on air.

Things weren't panning out for Norman. One of his lamps had sold, but the others were just sitting in the shop and soon were returned to him. He'd had another idea: he was making furniture out of plumbing materials. Beds, couches, chairs, all from copper pipes and brass fittings. I thought they were wonderful. He gave me a love seat for my new loft. Again shops had taken some pieces on consignment, but time passed, and they didn't sell.

I hadn't seen Norman for a couple of months when he showed up at my loft one day. "I gave up my place," he said. "I'm going back to Hydra." But first he was going to visit his mother out west. "Can I stay here until I leave?"

He was very depressed. He had no place to live. So I said okay, but just for a few days. He sat on my new love seat all day long, drinking, smoking, barely speaking. He was ruining my new sense of freedom. He was a downer. After three days I said he had to go, and he did. He disappeared from my life.

If I thought of Norman at all in the next months, I thought of him on Hydra. But about five months after he left, I got a letter postmarked Seattle. It wasn't from Norman, it was a notice from a mortuary. One of those printed "In Remembrance" cards.

I learned that Norman had been born on February 3, 1934. That he had died on November 12, 1978. That the service had been held at a Presbyterian chapel in Seattle three days later, and that the burial had been courtesy of the United States Army. Inside the printed mortuary notice was a handwritten note:

> Dorothy, it is so hard for me to write the sad news.
> Norman left a note asking me to notify his friends.
> He was with us 4 weeks. He had spent a few months at VA hospital in Maine. He said they had helped him.
> He was so depressed, & was leaving to go back on late plane on 12th. In the night his tragedy occurred.
> He left a long note saying his work was finished & could foresee no future. As yet I have not been able to accept it and am heartbroken . . .
> His mother . . .

So Norman had never gotten to Hydra. He'd had a ticket on a plane to New York. I wondered where he had been planning to stay, I wondered if he had been planning to call me for a place to stay. I wondered if he'd wondered what I would say. I wondered what he'd been thinking on the night of November 12, when he changed his mind.

A year or so later, I was startled to see furniture made of copper tubing and brass fittings in a high-end designer shop. I went in.

"These are very beautiful," I said. "Who made them?"

The shopkeeper named someone I had never heard of. He said that the furniture had been made from original designs by an artist. "Which artist?" I asked. He didn't know. I asked the prices: $2,000 for a double bedstead, $1,000 for a glass-topped coffee table. So. Norman's ideas had been good enough to rip off. Considering everything, I think he would have been glad to know that.

Rarely do I see Wendy's byline these days. When I come across it, I read her pieces with great interest; pleasure, in fact, since it doesn't seem to me that she's getting much help these days. Once in a blue moon, I run into Wendy herself. The last time we met was in a bookshop. She was very friendly.

"That was a brilliant piece you wrote about . . ." she said. "Why don't you call me? We can go for a walk in the park."

As we happened to be standing next to the cookbook section it occurred to me to mention that I'd solved the mystery of her missing *New York Times Cookbook*. Probably she hadn't had much occasion to refer to it during the two years I lived in her apartment. I had since learned that her copy had gone with the fleeing husband.

I hardly remember those days.

Mystery Woman Ruled Dead; Lost Since Break with Reds

A bizarre international mystery, with political under-themes, zig-zagging from Berlin to Moscow, ended its final chapter on an unsolved note yesterday as Juliet Stuart Poyntz, former American Communist leader, [was declared] legally dead.

—New York Daily Mirror,
FEBRUARY 13, 1944

On a long-ago afternoon I came home from school to find my mother sitting at the kitchen table. She was reading a newspaper. It wasn't one of the newspapers she usually read. In our house we read the *New York Post;* also *PM.* And *The Daily Worker.* I was intrigued, so I read over my mother's shoulder.

Who was she, this Juliet Poyntz? What was this mystery? Surely I asked my mother these questions.

And surely my mother would have said: "No one you knew, darling; it's not important." No one ever told me anything.

But over the years I sometimes recalled the feeling of consternation in our house that day—a flurry of telephone calls, low-pitched conversations. And when the time came, when I was ready to take an interest in the world that had so absorbed my family, I looked into the matter.

Let me begin here.

On May 28, 1936, less than a year before Juliet Stuart Poyntz disappeared, a woman, later described as young, attractive, blond, and Slavic-looking, went to the ticket counter at Chicago's Union Station. She told the ticket agent that her name was Mary Delmar, and in that name she bought a ticket for a lower berth to New York.

Certain things that followed from the purchase of that ticket are documented, others I can only surmise. I know, for instance, that Mary Delmar boarded the train, and that once she was aboard, she put on a pair of pajamas. I know that they were red pajamas. I assume that Mary Delmar, clad in her red pajamas, then lay down on her berth. And, presumably, as the wheels chugged and the whistle blew and the lights of towns flashed by, troubled thoughts kept Mary awake. Somewhere along the line, she made a decision, and when the train stopped to take on coal at Denholm, Pennsylvania, Mary Delmar, still wearing her red pajamas, jumped off. She left her suitcase behind and carried only two small things: a silver pocketknife with a man's name crudely scratched on it, and a photograph of a little boy.

Mary walked, ran, or stumbled some unspecified distance from the railroad tracks. At last she stopped, exhausted, and fell asleep in a clump of bushes at the edge of a horse pasture. At five o'clock on the morning of May 29, she was discovered by a local farmhand. He took her to the house of his employers, a family named Dolan, who gave Mary shelter.

For almost two weeks Mary remained with the Dolans. They may have been glad to have an extra hand, because in exchange for room and board, she was given chores around the house and garden. Sometime during those weeks, Mary came across Farmer Dolan's .22-caliber revolver. Maybe she hid it under her mattress for a few days while she thought about what to do. Maybe she made an immediate decision. Whichever, on June 13 she went out to the garden, picked some flowers, and tied her legs together with black ribbon. She then placed the flowers between her feet and shot herself in the right temple.

Luckily (or not, considering what was to come), Mary Delmar survived. The Dolans took her to Lewistown Hospital, where she was treated for an eye injury; possible brain damage was diagnosed. The nurses and interns at the hospital thought she was a mental case, but one Dr. Brown was not so sure.

"She answers questions very well," Dr. Brown wrote in his report, "until you come to the point where you begin to question her concerning her past life, when she immediately develops a headache and does not recollect." Dr. Brown believed that "she has some connection that she does not wish to divulge," and that she may be "communistic," as she had no use for the rich.

No doubt Mary Delmar has had a nervous breakdown. But she is in enough control of her emotions to hide what she wants to hide. It will develop that her real name is Rywka Brokowicz. And soon she will have a visitor—one Amy Mac-Master, a woman to whom she was previously unknown, and in whose custody she will be released from the hospital.

Juliet Poyntz now enters the story. It turns out that Amy MacMaster is acting on Poyntz's behalf. The FBI suspects that Delmar—or Brokowicz, as I will now call her—is a woman known to them as Lena. They believe that Lena is the Soviet recruiter of, and contact for, Juliet Poyntz.

Rywka Brokowicz will soon drop out of this story, but let's follow her as far as possible. At Poyntz's request, and for a payment of $25 a week to cover expenses, Amy MacMaster takes charge of Brokowicz. Eighteen years later, MacMaster will tell the FBI that she took Brokowicz home with her to Washington, D.C. But, unable to deal with the distraught woman, she placed her in a Philadelphia hospital. When Poyntz came to visit, Mac-Master witnessed Brokowicz becoming violently agitated.

Poyntz took over the situation. She obtained passports for MacMaster and Brokowicz and booked passage for them on the *Normandie,* sailing for France. She arranged for the two women to be accompanied on the ship by Dr. Julius Littinsky and his wife, Tilly. The foursome set sail on September 2, 1936. When they arrived in Paris, MacMaster remained with her companions for three days; then, leaving Brokowicz with the Littinskys, she returned to the States. Poyntz had told MacMaster not to worry; the Littinskys would turn Brokowicz over to "friends from Poland."

Who are the Littinskys? When questioned by the FBI in 1953, they will reluctantly acknowledge that Poyntz did ask them to befriend the two women, but they claim that they had only the most casual contact on the ship and, once in Paris, did not see the women at all. At the time he makes this statement, Dr. Littinsky is chief medical examiner for the International Workers Order and treasurer of the Morning Freiheit, both institutions closely associated with the Communist Party. He denies, however, that he was ever a Communist. He and his wife, Tilly, say they barely knew Poyntz, although Mrs. Littinsky thinks she saw Poyntz on the pier the day they sailed for France. The Littinskys also say that the purpose of their trip abroad in 1936 was to celebrate their twentieth wedding anniversary; after a brief stay in Paris, they had traveled by train through Germany and Poland and then on to the Soviet Union, where they visited relatives.

Goodbye to Rywka Brokowicz. We can hope that she was merely an unstable woman to whom Juliet Poyntz extended a disinterested helping hand; and that once in Poland, or wherever she landed, Rywka was reunited with the little boy whose photograph she carried from the train. Faint hope. This was 1936; by then Juliet Poyntz had been recruited as a Soviet agent, and she had shepherded Rwyka to the East just as the terror of Stalin's purges were about to peak.

Juliet Poyntz was an American girl born in Omaha in 1886. She was extremely well educated for any time, but particularly for her own. She earned an undergraduate degree from Barnard and a master's degree from Columbia University, and she won a fellowship for further study at the London School of Economics and Oxford. She was intelligent and high-minded. Early in her undergraduate days, she had become interested in social questions, particularly in matters of poverty and immigration, and in 1909 she joined the Socialist Party.

Photographs taken when she was a young woman show that Poyntz was an attractive woman, though somewhat spoiled for beauty by a heavy jaw. By all accounts she had compelling light brown eyes, a charming smile, and impressed everyone she met by the force of her character, her self-confidence, and her incisive intelligence. While she was studying in England, Poyntz met Friedrich Franz Ludwig Glaser, the heir to a German industrial fortune. Poyntz and Glaser came back to the United States together in 1913 and were soon married. The marriage lasted only a few years, but they never divorced and were still legally married in 1935, when Glaser died.

By the time Poyntz was forty, she was a personage in the world of radical politics. She had taught history at Columbia University, coauthored a book about the labor movement, been appointed director of education for the International Ladies' Garment Workers' Union, lectured for the Socialist Party, joined the Communist Party in 1921, and was a teacher at the Communist Workers' School. In 1924 the Party ran her as a candidate for Congress.

Everyone in the Party knew Poyntz. Whittaker Chambers, attending his very first Party meeting in 1925, left an indelible glimpse of Poyntz as she was in her late thirties: a heavyset, handsome, softly feminine woman who rose from her seat during the meeting to answer the remarks of the previous speaker. Calmly, and with impressive authority, she made the observation "The comrade is a liar."

For Party members, there was no such thing as an honest difference of opinion. A few months earlier, Poyntz had had this fact impressed on her. Finding herself on the losing side of one of the Party's internecine battles, she had been accused of "crimes of the highest order." At one point her views attained the status of an ism, as when the Party called for the liquidation of "Poyntzism." Her closest comrades, who had also backed the wrong side, were expelled. Poyntz was allowed to remain, but only after she had disavowed her previous views and sworn that from that moment on, she would follow the policies of the Comintern, no matter her own inclinations. In the years that followed, she was placed at the forefront of the Party; she ran for various public offices on the Party ticket; she frequently addressed cheering crowds and lectured to admiring students, none more attentive and admiring than the darkly pretty young woman who was my mother-to-be.

With all her many occupations, Poyntz often found time to travel abroad. Between 1921 and 1936, she applied for and received six passports: four in the name of Poyntz, two in the name of Glaser. In each passport application, she swore that her previous passport had been lost or, alternatively, that she had never been issued a passport. In her 1929 application, for instance, she wrote that the passport issued to her the previous year "was packed with numerous papers and books in a hurry and therefore carelessly in a rickety trunk that has been moved several times since last year . . . and evidently dropped out of the broken end of the trunk to my great regret since I have to pay $10 for a new one . . ."

Six passports are a lot of passports for one person. We would not be deviating from known facts if we were to infer that Poyntz's superfluous passports were turned over to Soviet-trained forgers and used as "boots" by comrades who preferred not to travel legally—specifically to the Soviet Union, or on Soviet business.

Poyntz was, herself, spending a significant amount of time in the Soviet Union. How do we know this? In August 1931, a flyer posted in Terre Haute, Indiana, advertised her as a lecturer who offered "the opportunity of a lifetime to hear about the wonders of WORKERS RUSSIA by the most brilliant woman speaker in the American labor movement WHO HAS JUST SPENT A YEAR IN SOVIET RUSSIA."

On April 8, 1934, using a passport issued in the name of Juliet Glaser, Poyntz sailed aboard the *Europa* on the first leg of another journey to Moscow. When she returned home early in the fall, friends noticed a change in her behavior. No longer was she the public face of the Party; nor did she attend Party meetings anymore.

She was not in hiding: friends and acquaintances ran into her from time to time and she was perfectly cordial. But she kept an uncharacteristically low profile, and those who knew how to read the signs believed that she had been recruited for "special work," which meant she was now an agent of Soviet intelligence.

In the mid-thirties, Poyntz lived in a brownstone apartment on the windswept corner of Seventy-fourth Street and Riverside Drive. She sometimes gave parties there, specifically to meet Columbia students; she also frequented the university's International House. She particularly wanted to become acquainted with Italian and German students, whom she attempted to recruit as agents to work for the Soviets when they returned home.

Elizabeth Bentley, who was a member of the Party and had spent some time as a student in Italy, was among those approached by Poyntz. Bentley was suspicious of Poyntz and refused her suggestion that she work in Italy with the anti-Fascist underground. But Poyntz had not been far off the mark in thinking the young woman was a likely recruit: Bentley would later work for the Soviet agent Jacob Golos, as a courier to a Washington spy network that included Alger Hiss; after Golos died, she ran the network herself. In 1945, when Bentley confessed her activities to the FBI, she told them among much else (including the name of a Julius who turned out to be Julius Rosenberg) of having been approached several times by Juliet Poyntz. But by that time Poyntz was eight years gone.

In October 1936—a little over a month after she stood on the pier, watching as Rwyka Brokowicz sailed to her fate on the *Normandie*—Poyntz, using her most recently issued Juliet Glaser passport, sailed once more, probably to the port of Riga, in Latvia, to make her way to Moscow. Think of it: Moscow in the winter of 1936–37. The first of the purge trials had taken place the previous August, ending with the death penalty for all defendants. The second wave of terror was about to burst, and this time it would include Stalin's agents in foreign countries, many of whom had received a summons "home."

Whittaker Chambers was called "home" to Moscow in 1937; he stalled and began to plan his defection. Ignatz Reiss, a high-ranking NKVD agent who had worked for Soviet intelligence in Spain, was called "home," broke with Stalin instead, and was assassinated in Switzerland. Walter Krivitsky, another high-ranking agent, defected after Reiss's murder and was found dead in mysterious circumstances in Washington a few years later. Theodore Stepanovich Mally, a Hungarian who had served the Soviet cause since World War I, was summoned "home." Ignatz Reiss's wife asked Mally why he was going to certain death. Out of guilt, he told her: guilt for the terrible things he had seen and done in Stalin's service. Jacob Golos, Elizabeth Bentley's superior, also stalled when he was recalled, and managed to die of natural causes.

Poyntz must have been filled with trepidation when she sailed that October. Miraculously, she returned to New York in February. She had escaped death. But, as she told an old friend, the anarchist and longtime anti-Stalinist Carlo Tresca, her faith had been shaken. While she had been in Moscow, her own loyalty had been questioned; somehow she had managed to allay suspicion but had been assigned to interrogate others. No doubt, like other interrogators, she learned how false confessions were obtained. To another old friend, Ludwig Lore, who had been expelled from the Party years earlier, she said that it no longer seemed possible for her to continue with underground work. She didn't know what to do.

Poyntz made no public statement of disaffection. She believed that she had a little time to figure things out—seven months, in fact. According to the return ticket found among her belongings, she had a third-class reservation aboard the *Britannic*, due to sail from New York on September 18, 1937. She was expected back "home."

On leaving New York in October, Poyntz had given up her apartment on West Seventy-fourth Street. She now lived in a studio apartment at the American Women's Association Clubhouse, on Fifty-seventh Street, near Tenth Avenue.

Toward the end of May 1937, Poyntz went to see her lawyer, Elias Lieberman. She told him that she was badly in need of money. Her husband, Friedrich Glaser, had died two years previously, and Poyntz, as his widow, was trying to collect from his estate. Lieberman told Poyntz that he thought he could get her an advance of about $1,000 from the estate. He would probably have the money for her by early June.

During the last week of May and the first days of June, Poyntz was seen in New York by a number of people: Carlo Tresca, whom she had met by chance and to whom she had confided her disillusion; Ludwig Lore, whom she saw frequently; Sophia Theis, another old friend, who later told the FBI that she had lunched with Poyntz in late May. Poyntz had told her, "I have extricated myself from my former connections and I am now going to do some writing." When Poyntz and Theis parted after lunch, they made a date to meet two weeks later.

On June 4, Poyntz had an appointment with a Dr. Worcester that she failed to keep. Elias Lieberman expected to hear from her that week about the money she desperately needed. She did not call him, and he was unable to reach her by phone. Lieberman was accustomed to her habits of travel, which was why, he told police, he did not report her missing for six months.

It was December 1937 when Lieberman, pressured by other friends of Poyntz's, finally went to the police. A detective was sent to Poyntz's apartment. He found her clothes hanging in the closet, her lingerie folded in the drawers, her luggage empty, her passport in a desk drawer. A bowl of Jell-O had long since gone to liquid on the kitchen table. Her trunks, which she had stored at a warehouse, contained only books and notebooks that outlined material for a projected history of modern Europe.

In mid-December a report of Poyntz's disappearance appeared in the New York newspapers. A reporter asked the Communist Party for a comment; the Party's New York State membership secretary said there was no record that the woman had ever been a member of the Communist Party.

Not another word was ever heard of Juliet Poyntz. The switchboard operator where she lived reported that a man with a deep voice, who had often telephoned her, did so again on the morning she disappeared. Soon after that phone call, Poyntz left her apartment. A year later, a grand jury was convened to hear testimony on her disappearance. A number of people had theories to offer—especially that she had been lured by an old lover to a Russian ship then docked in the harbor. As it turned out, no solid leads developed, and the investigation reached a dead end. Not many months later, the Soviet spymaster Colonel Boris Bykov rhetorically asked his agent Whittaker Chambers, "Where is Juliet Stuart Poyntz?" Delighted with his mastery of the American idiom, Bykov answered himself gaily, "Gone. Gone with the wind."

Seven years later, Poyntz's sister went to court to have Juliet declared legally dead. Very few details of the above story were known to my family, but enough were suspected to cause consternation in our house.

Jury Duty

On the morning of September 10, 1976, Jerome B. Mandel was sitting at his desk in his small beige-painted office in downtown Brooklyn. He was doing some paperwork on one of his cases, and he was hoping that his phone would ring.

Jerome (Jerry) was a criminal defense lawyer, a lone practitioner, small-time. Jerry himself was quite small, if pigeon-plump. And if he hadn't been to an Ivy League law school, and he didn't get the big-money cases, he was nevertheless a member of the bar, and his job was—as defense lawyers like to put it when they appear on television—to put the prosecution's proof to the test. This is a good job. It's mandated by the Constitution.

On that morning of September 10, Jerry Mandel's phone did ring. The conversation went something like this:

"My boy's in trouble."

"What kind of trouble?"

"They're saying he killed somebody."

Jerry Mandel reached for his yellow legal pad: the boy's name was Mark Simon, age seventeen; the victim was Charlie Houston, age twenty; the place was Morningside Park, in Harlem; the name of the investigating homicide detective was Robert Abrahamsen. Mandel got a sense of this case, which was similar to other cases he had handled, and in the course of this first conversation, he mentioned his fee. Experience had taught him that in cases like this, you'd better get your money up front.

September 8, 1976 (two days before Mandel's phone rang), was a hot, sunny day, just cooling off a little in the late afternoon. Mark Simon, who was known as Spooky to his friends, was riding around his Harlem neighborhood on a ten-speed bike. At about five o'clock, he turned the corner of his home block, which was 114th Street, between Eighth and Manhattan avenues. It must be said that these were bad years for the city; the crime rate was soaring, the streets were full of uncollected garbage, the infrastructure was in a general state of decay. As usual, things were worse in black neighborhoods than they were in the rest of the city, and that particular stretch of Eighth Avenue was burned out and vandalized. But 114th Street was mostly habitable, lined with six-story tenements, only a few of which were abandoned.

At that hour, and in such fine weather, there was a lot of activity on 114th Street. Children were playing games outdoors, windows were wide open, and women leaned out to shout to their children or call to neighbors on the stoops below. At a row of garbage cans on the east end of the block, four or five boys were gathered, among them Charlie Houston and his younger brother, Ben. Mark Simon knew them. He stopped his bike.

"Can I have a ride, Spooky?" said twenty-year-old Charlie Houston.

Mark agreed and handed over the bike. Charlie mounted, rode off, and returned a minute or two later. It was clear to everyone why he had come back so soon: the bike's rear tire had gone flat. Who was responsible for this? Charlie and Spooky exchanged angry words. Manhood was impugned. There were demands for money. Pushing and shoving occurred. The situation was not resolved.

A couple of hours later and a couple of blocks to the west, in the raised cement play area of Morningside Park, an area that runs between 116th and 119th streets, a basketball tournament was in progress. A few minutes after seven o'clock, when the games were in the last minutes of play, gunshots were heard. The games stopped. Heads swiveled toward the sounds. Clamorous voices distilled into screams.

Later, it would be estimated that between 70 and 150 people—spectators and players—filled the basketball courts that day. But when witnesses were questioned, only a few would admit that they had noticed anything unusual. One witness reluctantly agreed to talk to the police. His name was Lynwood Hicks.

Hicks, who was acting as a coach for one of the teams, said that he had heard the shots, looked up, and saw a man running toward the 119th Street end of the courts. The running man took a zigzag course, bumping against the fence as he ran (a cyclone fence surrounded the park), trying to evade the gunshots. He was evidently headed toward a large hole cut in the fence near the north end of the park.

As for the shooter, his physical description varied, depending on the witness. But all witnesses agreed with Lynwood Hicks to this extent: that as the victim tried to escape through the hole in the fence, the shooter crouched, took a two-handed grip on his gun (a black gun? a silver gun? a .38-caliber? a .45?), aimed deliberately, and fired again.

By that time the victim had reached the hole in the fence. He disappeared from view, having jumped or fallen to the sidewalk several feet below. And then, said Lynwood Hicks, the shooter tucked his gun into his belt, turned south as the crowd parted for him, and walked swiftly out of the park. The incident was over. The light was failing. The players resumed the game.

About twenty minutes later, Officer Robert Paz arrived at the park. He found Charlie Houston's body under a lamppost, below the hole in the fence. Charlie's pockets contained $18 and change; no weapon, or anything else of significance, was found on or near the body.

At about that moment, Charlie Houston's younger brother, Ben, was once again on 114th Street. As Ben sat on the lid of one of those garbage cans, he saw Spooky walking toward him from the direction of Morningside Park. Mark Simon didn't stop, but he slowed, and as he approached Ben, he glanced at him and muttered:

"I shot Charlie, but not to kill him."

So that was Jerry Mandel's case. Not an untypical case in a year when there would be more than 1,600 murders in the city. What was this one about? About a perceived insult to manhood? About a flat tire that could have been fixed with two or three dollars? About nothing. Or everything, depending on local codes of behavior. I'm told there are blood feuds in the Balkans that get passed along from generation to generation, until no one alive can recall the original dishonor. Anton Chekhov once wrote to his brother, "People must not be humiliated, that is the main thing."

In this case, the bar for humiliation seemed to be set pretty low, and the deeds required to maintain respect—or primacy—on the streets of Harlem pretty extreme. Still, Harlem is not some mountain fastness; almost everywhere, murder is considered the great human transgression. And when a killer is brought to trial, it is the great human drama. Citizens are summoned to render justice (or, if you like, to write the end of the play). In any case, I was summoned.

Mark Simon sat at the defense table, cloaked in the presumption of innocence. He was barely eighteen, a very dark-skinned boy, about five-seven, well built, broad through the shoulders, his hair worn in a well-trimmed medium Afro. On that first day, as through most of the trial, he slumped or lolled in his chair, pretending ease. The only sign of fear could be read in his lips, which moved constantly as he chewed on the inside of his mouth.

Next to him sat his lawyer, my first sight of the aforementioned Jerome Mandel. (I must tell you that if I seem to know more than a juror would be able to glean at a trial, it is because I was dissatisfied, consumed with curiosity about the hints of background events that never made it into open court. In short, I developed doubts about the verdict. So when the trial was over, I asked Jerry Mandel and Robert Abrahamsen and the prosecutor, Lothar Genge, to tell me what had been left out of the evidence on which the jury based its decision.)

• • •

When Charlie Houston's brother, Ben, heard Mark Simon mutter his confession—"I shot Charlie, but not to kill him"—he went to the police. That same night, Ben, together with homicide detective Robert Abrahamsen, searched the neighborhood, looking for Mark Simon. They didn't find him that night or the day after. But on September 10, Jerry Mandel placed a call to Robert Abrahamsen.

"I hear you're looking for my client," Mandel said. "You've got the wrong guy." Mandel repeated what Mark Simon had told him: "My client says a guy named Donny Wilkens was the shooter."

As it happened, on the fateful night of September 8, Donny Wilkens, who was a tall, husky young man, had flagged down a gypsy cab for a ride across town. When the cab stopped for a red light on Lenox Avenue and 116th Street, two men approached the cab and shot Donny Wilkens fifteen times, killing him instantly.

Abrahamsen wasn't buying the Donny Wilkens story. Later, he said, "Donny Wilkens was a bad actor. He had a lot of enemies. His killing was supposed to be over an argument he'd had about a girl earlier that day. I didn't think he had anything to do with Charlie Houston's murder."

Abrahamsen wanted Mark Simon, and three days later Mandel surrendered his client. Abrahamsen asked Mark Simon if he wanted to make a statement.

"No, sir," said Mark Simon.

Abrahamsen arrested him for the murder of Charlie Houston. The next day Mark Simon was arraigned and was back on the street on $5,000 bail.

Abrahamsen started looking for witnesses among the people who had been at the basketball court. Most of them said they had seen nothing. Abrahamsen was skeptical, to say the least: "A

Harlem kid has to notice. He's got to notice to survive. He's got to look at the guy with the gun so he can make sure he's not going to get it next. He's got to see which way the guy with the gun is headed so he can get out of the way. They know everything on those streets."

Eventually Abrahamsen came up with one eyewitness, a teenager named Howard James who lived in the neighborhood. Howard James said that he had seen Mark Simon shoot Charlie Houston on the basketball court. He was positive about it.

The other witness, Lynwood Hicks, was twenty years old. He was a college student, he had no criminal record, he did not live in the neighborhood, and he did not know Charlie Houston or Mark Simon or Donny Wilkens. Hicks was reluctant to tell Abrahamsen anything. He was scared. Nevertheless, he described the shooter as short, slightly built, dark-complexioned, and between twenty and thirty years old. The shooter had worn his hair in a close-cropped Afro, and he'd been armed with a large black gun. He might have been wearing a green jacket, but Hicks was not positive. When Hicks was shown an array of photographs that included Mark Simon and Donny Wilkens, he was unable to make an identification. But the description he gave of the shooter more closely resembled Mark Simon than Donny Wilkens, who was taller, huskier, older, and wore distinguishing sideburns and a beard.

With the positive identification from Howard James and Ben Houston's statements, a prosecutor was assigned to the case. This was Lothar Genge, who presented the case to a grand jury. On October 1, the grand jury handed down an indictment charging Mark Simon with murder.

• • •

Genge and Detective Abrahamsen were now working closely together. They both knew that with only one eyewitness identification, the case was weak. Abrahamsen continued trying to find other witnesses: "Ben Houston told me that a guy named Richard had been standing right next to him when Mark Simon said that he'd shot Charlie. Ben said that Richard had heard the confession. So I reach out for Richard. And Richard says he doesn't want to get involved. He doesn't own up to being there."

Instead of talking to Abrahamsen, Richard called Jerome Mandel.

"One day in January I get this call: 'Hey, man, this is Richard.' He's calling from a phone booth, and he tells me that Abrahamsen has been hassling him to be a witness, and that Ben is putting pressure on him too. So I say to him, 'Come on down to my office!' Because if the D.A. wants to talk to Richard, I sure want to hear what the guy's got to say."

Richard told Mandel that although he had not actually overheard Mark Simon's confession, Ben had repeated it to him just after it was made. Mandel was not happy, but things could be worse: "It wasn't admissible evidence; it's hearsay."

Mandel called Lothar Genge: " 'I hear you're looking for Richard. He's in my office now.'

"Genge nearly dropped dead," Mandel said gleefully. "His new witness turns up at my office! I told Genge what Richard said, and Genge said, 'I don't care what he says. I'm going to have him picked up as a material witness.' "

Lothar Genge, as tall and pale and thin as Mandel was short, dark, and plump, had been with the D.A.'s office for eight years, and he had some experience with reluctant witnesses. "Richard insisted that he had not actually overheard the statement, but who knows? What he did say was that just after Mark Simon passed by the garbage can where Ben Houston was sitting, Ben came over to him and told him what Mark had said: 'I shot Charlie, but not to kill him.' Richard said that Ben was really shaken."

The rules of hearsay evidence are too complicated for a layperson to understand, but in this case Genge couldn't introduce Richard's statement, even though it was confirmation of Ben's testimony. Still, Richard's statement increased Genge's confidence in his case.

"I never thought Ben had made up that confessional statement of Mark Simon's," Genge said. "It was too subtle; it exonerated Mark Simon of the legal charge of murder, while it still implicated him in the shooting. Ben wasn't capable of that. And here was Richard, who in no way wanted to get involved, who admitted to hearing about the confession immediately afterward."

On the night of Charlie Houston's death, Abrahamsen had been given the name of another possible eyewitness: a nineteen-year-old named Evelyn. Evelyn had two children who lived with Evelyn's mother in the Bronx. Evelyn lived wherever she could. "She'd call her mother every couple of days to see how her kids were, but she never went home. She'd live here one day, then pick up and move," Abrahamsen said. After hearing her statement, he brought Evelyn to Genge's office.

"Evelyn was not what you'd call an ideal witness," Genge said. "She had a record. She'd also been known to call herself Sharon Tate. But about this incident, she was very clear, very definite."

Evelyn had been at the basketball court; she had seen the shooter. He came into the park by himself. She saw him take a shot at Charlie while Charlie was playing basketball, just as Howard James had described. She saw Charlie running the zigzag course that Lynwood Hicks had described. Then she saw the shooter crouch, take the two-handed grip, and fire twice more with a black gun. She saw him only in profile, but her description matched the description Hicks had given—a short, slight young man with broad shoulders, wearing a light green jacket, his hair in a short Afro. Evelyn thought he was younger than the twenty-to-thirty age range Hicks had given. She thought he was about seventeen.

Abrahamsen tested her on the age question. "How old do you think I am?" he asked.

"Thirty-five," Evelyn said, getting it right.

But when Evelyn was shown an array of twelve photographs that included pictures of Mark Simon and Donny Wilkens, she picked out Donny Wilkens without hesitation. She said that Wilkens had been in the park. She knew him. Wilkens had once raped her girlfriend. And because she knew Wilkens and was terrified of him, she kept her eye on him. Wilkens, who had been wearing a black leather jacket and a white baseball cap, had left the park a few minutes before the shooting. He was definitely not the shooter, she said. But she wasn't sure that Mark Simon was either; in the photograph she was shown, Mark's hairline was different from her memory of it.

All exculpatory evidence must be turned over to the defense, and since Evelyn was unable to identify Mark Simon, Genge gave her name to Mandel.

"Evelyn cut both ways," Mandel said. "She couldn't identify Mark, but she said Donny Wilkens wasn't the shooter. If the
prosecution had brought her on as a rebuttal witness, I'd have
screamed objections: 'How did she know Donny had raped her
girlfriend? Was she there?' I was prepared to neutralize her testimony."

But Evelyn never testified at the trial. Soon after her name
was given to Mandel, she stopped returning Abrahamsen's calls
and couldn't be found.

The prosecution had one last bit of information. At about
eight P.M. on the night of Charlie Houston's death, a boy
named David was standing in front of the Golden Skillet restaurant on 114th Street and Eighth Avenue. He'd seen Mark
Simon, Mark's friend Otis Rivers, and a third person get into a
gypsy cab.

In the months before the trial, Jerome Mandel waited for his
client's witnesses to appear. "My client assured me that he had
witnesses who would testify that he wasn't the shooter." Mandel
was still waiting at the end of December, when Genge starting
pushing the case for trial.

"Genge starts screaming that we should raise my client's
bail. He's saying his witnesses are being threatened. He says, 'We
don't want these people down on the streets settling it among
themselves. Let's have a quick trial.'

"Well," Mandel said, "I didn't want that. I wasn't ready
for trial. Frankly, I didn't have the witnesses at that point."

At last Mark Simon produced three witnesses: Rafael, who
said he'd been told by Donny Wilkens himself that Wilkens had

shot Charlie; Otis Rivers, who said he'd seen Donny shoot Charlie; and Matty, who said that he too had seen Donny shoot Charlie. Mandel felt confident that, with two definite eyewitnesses who exonerated his client, he had a strong case. In February, Mandel's case became even stronger when Howard James, the only witness to positively identify Mark Simon as the shooter, recanted his testimony.

Genge was furious. "Now Howard is telling me that yes, he'd been in the park playing basketball, but that he never actually saw Mark Simon shoot the gun. He had come forward only because everybody in the neighborhood knew that Spooky did it."

Abrahamsen thought he knew very well what was going on. "This kid, Howard, is a fearful-type kid. Timid. I don't see him giving testimony that's a lie, but I can see him changing his mind when the guy he's testifying against is out on the streets. Bail has a dual function. It's supposed to protect society too. How are you going to conduct an investigation when witnesses are scared?"

What was Genge going to do? "Given the evidence we had even after Howard James recanted, I felt morally compelled to go to trial. Somebody had been killed. I felt I had legally sufficient evidence, but I wasn't sure a jury would be satisfied beyond a reasonable doubt."

The case was marked for trial in early February. Two days before, Mandel called Genge. To his surprise, Genge sounded "real blase about going to trial. I couldn't believe it! Was this the same Lothar who was gangbusters to start? I went up to his office, and he's, like, very depressed. He says to me, 'Look, frankly I haven't got much. Give me a good witness who says that Donny did it, and we won't go to trial.'"

Mandel decided that fourteen-year-old Matty, who said he had seen Donny Wilkens shoot Charlie, was his most credible witness. "I thought Genge would take Matty's statement and maybe throw the case out. But Matty messed around. I couldn't get him to go down to Genge's office."

While he waited for Matty to appear at his office, Genge read the notes of Mandel's interview with Matty. Matty had told Mandel that the shooting had taken place at the entrance to the basketball court, a statement that flatly contradicted both Lynwood Hicks and Evelyn, both of whom placed the shooter far into the court.

"Okay," Genge said to Mandel. "We're going to trial."

On Tuesday, March 1, the jury, my jury, began to hear evidence.

We would never hear Howard James identify Mark Simon as the shooter.

We would never hear Evelyn insist that Donny Wilkens was not the shooter.

We would never hear Richard confirm Ben Houston's statement about Mark Simon's confession; nor would we hear David testify that he had seen Mark Simon and Otis Rivers get into a cab together when both would claim to have been somewhere else. ("The last I heard of David," Genge told me, "he was in the intensive care unit of Harlem Hospital with stab wounds.")

Nor did Matty or Rafael—both of whom had told Mandel that Donny Wilkens was the shooter—testify for the defense. "Matty showed up for the trial," Mandel said later, "but he was spaced out. The kid was like a zombie, I couldn't put him on the stand." And Rafael? "He never showed up at all."

What was left of the case?

Ben Houston, Charlie's younger brother, was the first to take the witness stand. He gave his age as seventeen. He was a stocky boy; he spoke slowly. He said that at five P.M. on September 8, he was sitting on the lid of a garbage can on 114th Street when Charlie returned Spooky's bike with the rear tire gone flat.

"Spooky asked Charlie for three dollars to fix the flat. Charlie said he'd give Spooky two dollars. They kind of pushed the bike at each other. Then I said I'd pay to fix the tire. Spooky said to me, 'That's not the principle. God gave him a gift, and he didn't know how to use it. I'm gonna kill Charlie.' "

Shortly after the incident with the bike, Charlie went to Morningside Park to play basketball, while Ben rode the streets on his own bike for a while. Then he rode back to 114th Street to keep a date with a girl named Debbie Parker.

Debbie Parker was a pretty girl, only fourteen but she looked older, not the least bit nervous, in fact very self-possessed. She said that, yes, on September 8 she had walked over to 114th Street to meet Ben Houston. She was early for their date; while she waited for Ben, she saw Mark Simon talking to another boy. She knew Mark. She went over to him.

"Hi, how you feeling, Spooky? Haven't seen you for a long time."

Spooky paid no attention to her and kept talking to his friend.

"Spooky was saying that he'd almost just put Charlie to sleep, and if he had done it once, he'd do it again. He said he had a gun. He'd been going to throw it away, but now he wouldn't. He'd use it on Charlie."

The evening was gathering speed. Debbie left the block at

about seven-thirty. Fifteen minutes later, Ben Houston was once again hanging around the garbage cans when he saw Mark Simon walk quickly up the street, coming from the direction of the park, heading toward Eighth Avenue. Mark did not stop, but as he approached Ben, he slowed down and muttered a sentence just loud enough for Ben to hear:

"I shot Charlie, but not to kill him."

That evening, after he learned that Charlie was dead, Ben led Robert Abrahamsen, of the Fifth Homicide Zone, on a fruitless search of the neighborhood for Mark Simon.

Lynwood Hicks took the witness stand. Before beginning his testimony, he asked the judge if the door to the corridor could be closed; he didn't want to be seen. He was an impressive witness, twenty-one years old, a college student majoring in occupational therapy; he worked in a community methadone program, was an outsider to the neighborhood, and knew no one involved in the case.

"I was standing on the sidelines watching the team when I heard sounds, like firecrackers or shots. I looked toward the north end of the court and saw this guy running a zigzag course. I saw this other guy running after him. He took aim and fired again. I turned my head away. When I looked back, this guy, the shooter, was walking in my direction and tucking his gun into his belt. The gun was a large one, black, a thirty-eight, maybe a forty-five. I got out of his path."

Hicks described the shooter: about five-seven, broad shoulders, short Afro. When asked if he could identify the defendant as the shooter, Hicks looked directly at Mark Simon for the first time.

"I'm not sure."

• • •

After three days of prosecution witnesses, Mandel opened for the defense. He had found a new witness, one whose existence he was unaware of until the trial was already under way: Joshua Sullivan, eighteen, a high school student, well-spoken, with no arrest record. Joshua had gone to the basketball court on September 8. He said that he and a girl whose name he did not know entered the court through the hole in the north end of the fence. They had been watching the games for about five minutes when he heard the shots. He saw the shooter crouched about three yards away.

He had a silver gun. He was about five-ten and husky, with sideburns and chin whiskers.

"No," Joshua said to Mandel's question about whether he knew Donny Wilkens.

"Did you know the defendant?"

"Yes, but I only saw him a few times at the house of this girl I was dating. He was dating her sister."

At this point the jury exchanged perplexed glances: this was our first clue that Mark Simon's defense was going to be "some other dude did it." Although we had no way of knowing that Joshua Sullivan was a surprise witness, we could see that Genge was angry.

"Did Mr. Mandel take notes during your interview?" Genge asked the witness.

"Yes."

Genge turned to Mandel. "May I see those notes, Mr. Mandel?"

"Certainly, Mr. Genge."

Genge read through the yellow legal pad and faced the

witness again. "I see here in Mr. Mandel's notes that you described the shooter as having a mustache."

He handed the notes to Joshua Sullivan, pointing to the relevant lines.

"That must be a mistake," the witness said.

"Oh, by the way, Mr. Sullivan, you said that the shooter was about three yards away from you. How many feet is that?"

"I don't know."

The penultimate witness for the defense was Otis Rivers, who acknowledged that he was a good friend of Mark Simon's and was at the basketball court on the fatal day.

"I saw Donny Wilkens shoot Charlie Houston."

For a week the jury had been studying Mark Simon—furtively, because the connection between us was too charged to acknowledge by open staring. He looked very young. Except for his hair, which was now neatly styled in a medium Afro (grown out, one might conjecture, from the short Afro described by witnesses), he matched exactly the descriptions given of the shooter by the prosecution witnesses.

For a week he had seemed affectless, paying no attention to the evidence, whether helpful or damaging to his case. He lolled in his seat, occasionally whispered to Mandel, constantly chewed on the inside of his mouth.

And now he was taking the stand. For the occasion, he was more formally dressed than he had been, wearing a three-piece gray suit with white stripes, a dark shirt, and a light patterned tie. He was also wearing black-rimmed tinted goggles. The goggles and the outfit were a mistake; he looked older, more menacing. The jury could hear Mandel whisper to him to take off the glasses.

He was a heavily coached witness, which may also have been a mistake.

"Yes, sir . . . No, sir . . . That's correct, sir . . . Then we proceeded to the corner . . ."

In response to Mandel's leading questions, he told the jury about his life.

"I live at home with my mother, father, my brothers, and three puppies . . . No, I don't go to high school anymore. I used to go to Charles Evans Hughes High School, but my father got sick and I had to quit to work in his trucking business . . . Yes, sir, I'm studying at night for my high school diploma."

As for the events of September 8:

"Charlie asked me for a ride on my bike. Charlie was a bully. He was always picking on younger, smaller kids . . . Yes, sir, I was afraid of him.

"When Charlie brought my bike back with the flat, I asked him to fix it. He says, 'Nobody tells me what I got to do.'

"I say, 'I'm not telling you what you got to do. You asked me for a ride like a man, I give you a ride like a man, you should fix it like a man.' "

Mark Simon denied that Ben Houston was present during this exchange. As for Debbie Parker, there was no way she could have overheard any conversation he had that afternoon. And besides:

"I used to mess around with Debbie, and then I broke up with her. She's got an attitude about me. She's going with Ben now."

After the incident with Charlie and the bicycle, Mark asked his friend Otis Rivers to go to Morningside Park with him. He was upset; he wanted to play some basketball to take his mind off the argument with Charlie. As he and Otis walked toward the park, they were joined by two other friends, one of them Donny Wilkens. They continued toward the park, walking in pairs, Donny and Mark together. Mark told Donny about his argument with Charlie. Donny shook his head and mentioned that he too had been in a fight that day. He said, "I just don't know what's happening with these guys. I just been hit across the dome piece with a baseball bat."

When the four friends arrived at the park, they stood on the sidelines watching the games. Soon Charlie Houston approached them with a basketball under his arm.

"I see you brought your crew with you," Charlie said to Mark.

"It's not like that," Mark replied.

Donny intervened. He said to Charlie, "Don't you ever get tired of messing with people? Why don't you pick on somebody your own size?"

"Don't pay him any mind. He's not worth it," Mark said, pulling at Donny's arm.

"I'm getting tired of him," Donny said as Charlie walked away. "I'm going to take care of it."

Donny followed Charlie. Mark saw them facing each other, taking threatening postures; he heard their voices raised. He saw Charlie lift the basketball he was carrying, as if to throw it in Donny's face. Donny stepped back a pace, took a pearl-handled silver gun from his belt, and shot at Charlie. As Charlie started running away, Mark and Otis Rivers quickly left the park.

"How did you feel about what happened?" Mandel asked.

"I felt bad. I felt like it was my fault, sir."

Once out of the park, Mark said, he and Otis Rivers separated. Mark headed down toward 110th Street, where his current girlfriend lived. But when he got to her house, no one was at home. He waited for about a half hour and then, still upset, he took a cab to a movie theater on Third Avenue and Eighty-sixth Street. When he got out of the movie, he called home. His mother answered the phone and said, "The police have been here looking for you. Better not come home. Go to your sister's house in Brooklyn. We'll get you a lawyer."

Mandel had attempted a portrait of a responsible young man, one who lived in a stable family with brothers and sisters and puppies, one who left school to help in his incapacitated father's business, who eagerly studied at night for his high school diploma, who was fearful of the neighborhood bully. Now it was Genge's turn for cross-examination, and he pretty much destroyed Mandel's presentation. Genge offered Mark Simon as a heroin dealer who had been arrested and convicted for possession. Then Genge submitted two documents from Mark Simon's former high school: one from a teacher who reported that Mark Simon had slapped her across the face; the other from an assistant principal who said that Mark had threatened her. It was for these offenses that he had been suspended from school.

Genge handed Mark the conviction sheet and the two school reports.

"Those things never happened," Mark Simon said.

Mandel's closing argument tried to wrap up all the loose ends. Ben Houston, Mandel said, knew that Donny Wilkens had murdered Charlie. It was Ben himself who had killed Donny in revenge. And then, Mandel suggested, Ben had decided that

On April 14, Mark Simon was back in the courtroom for sentencing. So were some of his friends and family. So were Mandel and Genge. So was I.

Mandel made a plea for a sentence of five years' probation on the grounds that Mark Simon was a youthful offender. The judge denied it. Mark Simon made his own plea for probation. He said that he wanted to help raise the baby his girlfriend was soon going to give birth to. The judge denied it.

Mark Simon was sentenced to nine years. At that time a nine-year sentence translated into a third of the time to be served in prison, with two thirds off for good behavior. So if he didn't get into trouble in jail, Mark Simon would probably be back on the street by the age of twenty-one.

I don't know anything about what happened to him after the day he told us about the baby who was going to grow up without a father.

Do you wonder if he took care of that baby when he got out of prison?

Do you wonder if he ever killed anyone else?

I sometimes wonder. I also wonder if, now that Mark Simon is forty-five, he's not a pillar of some community somewhere. That could happen. Or he could be dead.

All I know is that for a couple of weeks, his world and his young life opened to me. It was as if I had picked up a novel, a real page-turner, and while I read, the dishes piled up in the sink, the floor went unswept, the phone rang unanswered. I could think of nothing else until I'd finished the story. And when I reached the last page, I closed the book and put it on the shelf.

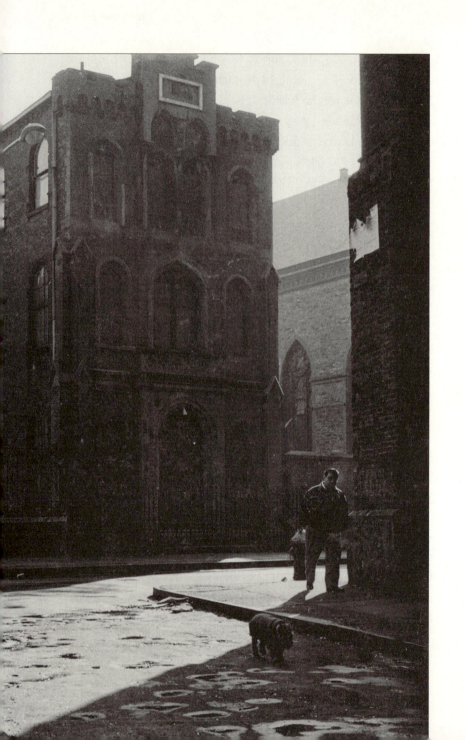

In the Vicinity of Art

The sign says Jersey Street, but that's too dignified a title for this leftover remnant of downtown real estate. Jersey Street is no more than an alley now, about as wide as the average living room, running two east-west blocks from Crosby Street to Mulberry. Sometimes you see a truck squeezing through, but no one lives on Jersey Street anymore.

I must have passed by Jersey a dozen times without noticing it. Then, one morning, as I was walking down Lafayette Street to have coffee on Prince Street, a shaft of early sun struck a brilliant diagonal down the alley. I glanced toward the sunlight. At that very moment a small white wirehaired dog trotted around the corner from Mulberry. The dog snuffled his way along the cobblestones, through sun and into shadow, headed for a puddle that had formed in a pothole; his short, squat owner waddled after him and stepped into the shaft of sun. At that moment—the decisive moment, as Cartier-Bresson named it—I raised my camera and took a picture. And what a beauty it turned out to be, with every tone that black-and-white film can render: the man outlined in sun; the dog halfway across the line from sun to shadow; the steel shutters of the buildings that usually darkened Jersey angled every which way, picking up glints of sun; and, in the background, still in soft shadow, the pretty chapel of Old St. Patrick's. If you ask me, this photograph is in the vicinity of art.

Of course, if you get onto the subject of art, everybody's a critic, and who am I not to have my own ideas? I like to look through those shoe boxes on flea market tables, the ones that overflow with the photographic detritus of lost lives. So often I'm struck by the beauty and the perfect framing of a snapshot. Is it art if it's an accident? Sometimes I see an image that is the definition of kitsch; as, for example, the postcard I bought of someone's beloved shepherd mutt. It was surely the dog's owner who had the snapshot hand-tinted and printed up as a postcard, and who, in 1912, stamped it, mailed it from Carson City, Nevada, and wrote the still-legible penciled message: "Please take good care of our dog." Imagine the narrative possibilities! A family flees town in the dead of night, leaving everything behind. To return? Never to return? What are their circumstances? What happens to them . . . to the dog? The postcard isn't art, but a writer who is touched by it might make art of it.

Or not.

I've been a critic, professionally. I've written reviews in my time, though never about fiction, certainly not about theater. I have my opinions about fiction and plays, but since I can't write either one, I don't feel competent to write about them. I write about nonfiction, on subjects I happen to know something about. I haven't always been kind to the writer. Sometimes a book just makes you mad.

But let's say that an old friend of mine, a dear friend, a playwright all his life, gets his play produced on Broadway. The play is highly acclaimed and my friend delights in his success. Since he is no longer as young as he once was, the moment is all the sweeter. He is sought out by interviewers who want to know about his play, and about his life. And often, when he gives these interviews, his wife, who is my best friend, is at his side. One day I come upon this passage in an interview he has given:

"Has the great success of your play had any effect on your life?" the interviewer asks my friend Nick.

"No, not really," Nick answers.

The interviewer has made no indication of it, but I'm pretty sure that at this point Nick will have paused and exchanged glances with Nora.

"But," Nick continues, "you learn that some of your friends rejoice at your good fortune, and others don't, which comes as a surprise and is painful."

As far as I know, there were no others who caused surprise and pain. There was only me. Mea culpa.

Listen, over the years I've lost lots of friends, to say nothing of other significant others. These things happen—people drift apart, irritations mount, an unforgivable betrayal occurs, whatever—there are dozens of reasons. But I never thought I'd lose Nick and Nora, and I couldn't have dreamed of the reason: I didn't like his play.

You didn't like his play? So *what*?

So what, indeed.

• • •

You know, I often wonder whether exceptionally attractive couples have a better time in bed than those of us of the more average persuasion. I suspect they do, don't you? Because in the Darwinian sense, they've hit the jackpot.

Nick and Nora were dazzling, anyone could see that. They were Olympian: tall, slender, beautiful, intelligent, witty. They were fifteen years into marriage when I met them, and crazy about each other, a dyad, not a sliver of separation between them. If they were poor, it was by choice. For art's sake, they had chosen poverty—if that was the way things went. All was not lost; art might yet provide.

Some of Nick's plays had been respectfully read, and some had been produced in off- and off-off-Broadway theaters. In the meantime they lived as cheaply as possible, earning money here and there at jobs that left Nick as much time to write as possible. Nick's life as a writer was the center of their lives, as much the center of Nora's life as it was of his. Not that there was anything recessive about Nora. *Au contraire.*

When we met—this would be in the mid-seventies—my circumstances were a little different. I wasn't married, not anymore. They had children, I had none. I was making a bare living writing freelance articles for women's magazines. My career ambitions were modest; I didn't think about being an artist. But we became friends, and along with lack of money, we had a number of other things in common: we agreed on politics, which included being against the Vietnam War and for civil rights, we held utopian hopes for a society organized on principles of justice, we had a tropism toward old-fashioned bohemianism. Also, we laughed at the same things.

But one thing was no laughing matter. Nick's genius.

One day early in our friendship, Nora said to me, "Nick is a genius."

She wasn't using the word lightly, as you might say to someone, "Oh, you found my glasses! You're a genius!" Or as you might use the word to mean that someone was really smart. No. Nora believed Nick was a genius; she didn't say that to everyone, she was making me a confidence. By implication, she was also telling me that not only had she chosen a genius, a genius had chosen her, which didn't make her chopped liver.

What did I think of it? I thought: Well, what do I know about genius? Einstein was a genius, but with my knowledge of physics, I had to take that on faith. Beethoven, Mozart, acknowledged geniuses, but I had a tin ear. Chekhov, Shakespeare: I know they were geniuses because I know how to read. Tom Stoppard: okay, yes. I had a good eye for painting (if it wasn't too abstract) and for photography, so I included Michelangelo and Cartier-Bresson and Saul Steinberg in my pantheon.

Nora gave me some of Nick's scripts to read. She gave me the script of his major unproduced play. I went with them to Alphabet City, where, on bare, unswept stages, actors sat around and read Nick's words. Was his genius apparent to me? Well, if enjoyment is a measure of greatness, I'd have to say that those experiences didn't give me much pleasure. But I felt handicapped: reading Nick's scripts, seeing them performed, made me nervous. Too much was at stake; our very friendship seemed to be at stake. And what I thought at the time was that I was too ignorant to understand the work. I assumed that what Nick was doing was beyond me—maybe it was avant-garde, maybe there was some aesthetic or literary principle that I just didn't get. Nick did what he did. So what if I didn't see the light? They were my friends.

It wasn't only Nora who thought Nick was a genius. This was something they agreed on, a foundation stone on which their marriage was built, and many of their friendships too. And even if the word "genius" took me aback, I had no doubts about Nick's intelligence, about his erudition. He was full of arcane knowledge, he read everything, he had large, complicated political and social theories, he could dredge up obscure, seemingly singular historical events and spin a cosmology that remade your understanding of the world. At least for the moment.

Nor was Nora a slouch. You should have heard them at dinner parties. They were a team, they flew on the wings of logic, and they never ever backed off an argument, especially not Nora, who could make mincemeat of anyone who disagreed. Argument was their delight, their sport. Sometimes a spectator sport.

Once in a great while, though, Nick would base an argument on a proposition that, by some fluke, I knew was flawed. Did I offer correction? Nope. I decided that I had probably misunderstood. Or, more accurately, I was afraid that my intellectual resources would drown in his deep water. And as for Nick's work, of course I praised it.

"Great," I said. "Great!"

Because isn't that what you say to a friend? And anyway I didn't have the nerve to say otherwise. Once, very tentatively, I asked Nora a question about one of Nick's plays—about a character who seemed less than plausible, or a plot line that confused me. Well, believe me, when I heard Nora's sigh of impatience, of contempt, really, I grew properly frightened. "I would grow properly frightened" is what Alfred Kazin said about his encounters with the mad Delmore Schwartz, not that I mean to imply Nora was mad. But fierce. Oh yes.

So you can see, can't you, that over the years these things accumulate? You dislike yourself for feeling intimidated: you become resentful of your friends, you blame your timidity on them when it's nobody's fault but your own. You draw back, you keep your reservations to yourself, you operate below the level of good faith. Mea culpa, as I said.

But don't forget that all this was sub-rosa. When these thoughts came to the surface, I pushed them away. I castigated myself for disloyalty. And for many years, we were having so much fun. Picnics, parties, a shared circle of friends. I had been floating in the world, unattached, and we became a threesome. They were the best of friends to me, loyal and loving friends. I published a book: they were happy for me. I had miserable love affairs: who else would I cry to? I had surgery: I counted on Nora. Our parents grew old and died: we went through that together. We went through life together.

And then Nick's luck began to change. One of his plays was produced off-Broadway and got good reviews. We four—by this time I had married—went to opening night together. We stood and cheered. We called, "Author, Author" as Nick took his bows. In fact, I had problems with the play—with Nick's style, which seemed self-conscious to me, with his language, which I thought self-insistent. I thought the situations and characters were contrived. It didn't matter. I was happy for them. Really. No reservations.

Nick was launched. He had a promise of a Broadway production for his new play. A year later it was finished. "It's genius!" Nora said to me. She was beside herself with happiness. She kept me au courant—and I mean several times daily—of each step in the production process: the stars who were eager for parts, the renowned director who had signed on, the producers who were investing big money. Everyone agreed: the play was genius . . . brilliant . . . thrilling . . .

I admit that I was getting a little nervous now. What if I didn't like it—and didn't I have reason to worry about that? The level of praise required for a major piece of work might be beyond my abilities. Also, I wanted to say, "Nora. Back off." I thought a little reticence on her part might be in order. I thought it might be a good idea for her to let the play speak for itself.

But reticence was not Nora's style, nor was "back off" mine. She was so certain, so convinced of Nick's genius; no one with an ounce of intelligence, an ounce of sensibility, could fail to see it for herself. Certainly not her best friend. Soon Nora had a treat for me. She put the script in my hands. She could barely wait for my expressions of joy.

Well, for the first ten pages or so, I felt huge relief. I thought, "Okay, this is good, this is working, I'm going to like this." But I read on and my heart sank.

There isn't much difference between reading a play and reading a novel. Reading is reading; when you're reading something good there comes a moment when the physical experience of looking at print dissolves and the work takes you over; you're deep into a journey. But reading a friend's work can never quite offer that experience. No matter how good the work is, disbelief can't be entirely suspended. You know the voice too well, you know where characters and events come from. As in this case. I knew where everything came from. These were not fictional characters to me. I knew them. I knew them as well as I knew my best friends. And I saw that the hero of my friend's play was a man who is a genius and something of a guru; also a moral giant who is generally irresistibly attractive to women, in particular to the beautiful heroine, who pursues him, understands and shares his qualities, and happens to be the only woman worthy of him.

What *was* my problem? Was this self-delight news to me? No. Nevertheless, I was shaken. When, in daily life, I find myself unsettled, I usually go shopping, but there is no distraction from art. They say that art can change you, and so it did. It was as if an optometrist had shifted lenses; in that split second I saw things differently. Of course, there were other elements to the play: the setting was imagined, the plot contained various interestingly imagined events. Still, my feelings had changed. I couldn't help it.

I was in despair, really.

"Great," I said. "It's just great!"

But I couldn't muster conviction. The play made me mad.

In view of subsequent events, you may legitimately ask me: "What do *you* know about art?" Because then the reviews came, prizes came, production companies were formed to take the play on the road, movie offers poured in. Yes, it *was* a great play! Everyone said so. And if I happened to miss a review, Nora sent it to me. My e-mail filled up with Nick's glorious reviews.

"Isn't this review wonderful?" Nora would e-mail. And I'd read the review and e-mail back, "Oh, yes. Wonderful." But I wasn't persuaded; I thought what I thought, and Nora wasn't fooled.

But this is what I kept asking myself: why should it matter?

Weren't Nick and Nora the same people, the same loyal and loving friends they'd always been? If, these days, in their happiness, there was some extra preening going on, a bit more holding forth at dinner tables, Nick's genius not such a tightly held secret anymore, so what? Wasn't euphoria perfectly natural?

But it did matter to me. And I asked myself what Nora later accused me of: was I jealous?

Because the time came when Nora said, "We know you've been resentful of Nick's success. You haven't been able to hide it . . . From the very moment of the first reviews you've made your feelings clear . . ." She held the moral high ground. Of course. What other ground does a wronged friend occupy?

I drank two martinis then. Gulp. Gulp.

Naturally that's what she would think. *They* would think. In their place I would have thought the same. You cast around for a reason why your best friend is not rejoicing in your happiness. What could it be? Jealousy. After all, wasn't I a writer too? Wasn't my husband a writer? Nothing like the acclaim that had come to Nick had been our portion.

But really I didn't think so, and how could I say what it was? It was fatigue. The long years of my own bad faith had exhausted me.

"You have a devil in you," Nora said.

I said, "I've ruined our friendship, haven't I?"

"Not if I can help it," said my generous real-life friend.

But I had. I felt sick.

Remember that photograph I took on Jersey Street? The dog, the man, sun and shadow. I was so pleased with it that I decided to do a series of Jersey Street pictures. Every day, or at least several times a week, in various weathers and different hours, I planned to stand on Jersey Street with my camera, just to see what passed by. I never did that.

Too bad. Because a while ago I found myself on the corner of Jersey Street again. For old times' sake, I stopped to look east toward Mulberry. It was a raw day in early spring. Fine rain fell from a polished pewter sky. At that very moment a nun in full regalia appeared on Mulberry Street. Three nuns followed behind her. Each nun carried a black umbrella. In the bright gray shadowless drizzle, they paraded in line past the pretty chapel of Old St. Patrick's. Think of it: four nuns in black-and-white habit; four black umbrellas held aloft; four umbrellas, four nuns, all tilted at identical angles into the wind. I didn't have my camera. In a moment they were gone. I felt sick. I had lost them.

Foucault's Last Lover

In the dead of winter, in the dark before dawn, my phone rang.

A slurred voice spoke: *"You . . . love . . . made you liter-ary executor . . . left everything . . . you . . . my will . . . look in typewriter . . ."*

Clonk.

Were I to write a screenplay for this scene, you'd see a woman lying in bed in a dark room, her form beguilingly outlined by the faint street light that penetrates her window. You'd hear rain beating on the window, and then the jarring sound of a ringing telephone: brrrr . . . brrrr . . . brrrr . . . At the third ring, the woman rouses herself; groggy with sleep, she switches on a bedside light and reaches for the phone.

The scene shifts. A man in a brightly lit room is sitting on the edge of a bed. He speaks into a telephone. The camera moves in for a close-up, closer, closer, until the hand grasping the phone fills the screen. You watch as his hand loosens its grasp; in slow motion, an empty pill bottle drops to the floor, and the phone falls from his now-lifeless fingers.

Clonk.

A woman's voice crackles from the receiver on the floor: "Goddammit, Keppel!"

"Keppel," my friend Kitty said. "You should meet Keppel."

Keppel had been at Swarthmore with Kitty's husband.

I said, "Really? Isn't he married? I heard he was gay. You think he'd be interested in me?"

"He's separated," said Kitty. "He's not gay. Of course he'd be interested in you."

I told her the old joke: "Just because he's married and has two children doesn't mean he's gay."

Kitty laughed politely. "Anyway," she said, "you're beautiful, you're smart, and you're both writers. You could just meet him."

Kitty loved her friends exceedingly: none of us was less than beautiful, none of us had ever held a half-empty glass, none of us had a problem that wasn't a blessing in disguise. Kitty was an optimist; if you were a pessimist, as I happened to be, Kitty's worldview could drive you up the wall.

But it was true that when she mentioned Keppel, I perked up. I'd liked his book, which had to do with class. Social Class. I hadn't actually read his book, but I'd read about it, so I knew it was the kind of book that a person like me—a person who aspired to seriousness—should like.

Kitty gave an elegant dinner party, and late in the evening, long after I'd lost hope of him, Keppel strolled in. He was coatless (it was winter), with a cashmere scarf draped casually over his tweed jacket. I must say that I was somewhat taken aback. I had imagined a tall, thin, dark-eyed aesthete. Keppel was not short, but his body was soft and fleshy. He had the pale, waxy skin that is (unfairly, no doubt) associated with not washing very often. He had a few strands of brown hair. Large tortoise-shell glasses magnified his eyes. Soon I heard him laugh, the overloud laugh that comes a moment too late, from a person who doesn't really have a sense of humor; and I heard his voice, which was pitched high, in the rhythm of complaint.

I decided to cut him a break. You know the saying "Handsome is as handsome does"? Ridiculous. Everyone knows that handsome gets away with murder. In fact, that very evening at Kitty's dinner party, there was a very handsome man, married, who was making friendly overtures to me. I knew that would end in tears. I was a grown woman and I was ready to take other factors into consideration. In academic circles, Keppel was a celebrated man, a serious intellectual. That was attractive. I gave him a few minutes to notice me. He didn't. I called myself to his attention.

"I loved your book," I lied. "I'm so interested in class—Class."

There's a lame come-on for you.

"How nice," he said. "Are you?" His eyes scanned the room.

"Yes," Kitty said. "You know Dorothy's written a book about Class too." She told him the title.

Keppel looked at me with some interest. "Oh, is that your book! I loved it." In time I would learn that he had never even heard of my book, which, in any case, had not put me in his distinguished class (lowercase). But, as I had been identified as a published person, I was worth another glance.

Thus we two (let's call us flatterers, not liars; not yet) shared a taxi downtown to our respective homes.

"We should have lunch," Keppel said.

"Great!" I said. "Here's my number."

I waited three weeks before I called him. It's not that I never call men, but I prefer vice versa. I have learned that when a man says he'll call you and your telephone is silent, that's the message. But as I said, I'd made a decision: a man like Keppel was just the sort of man I needed. On paper, he was perfect.

I dialed Keppel's number, hoping to get his answering machine. He was home. There was no hint of recognition in his voice, even after I had identified myself by my first name and my last name. I still had to mention where we had met.

"Oh," he said. "I was just about to call you."

Such good manners. We arranged to have dinner. Everyone called him Keppel. His mother had named him, or so he often said, after Karl Marx. With or without this provenance, Karl was a perfectly good name, but for some reason, people had settled on Keppel. There was something comical about the name. In Yiddish, *keppel* means "head." "What a *keppele* on that child!" grandmothers boast about their grandchildren. But can you imagine saying, "I love you, Keppel"?

I don't think I ever said it. Not even in our most intimate moments (of which, yes, there were some). If I did say it, I refuse to remember, even though, for about a year, we were sort of a couple, Keppel and I. These many years later, I look back at that time and see that I was in a constant state of expostulation.

"But *why* did you tell me that you were going to Chicago and then tell Michael that you were in Philadelphia? Were you even out of town at all?"

"When that woman said she'd been to Choate, why did you say *you'd* gone to Choate when you told me you'd gone to public school?"

"I never lie," Keppel would say serenely each time he was caught in a lie. He lied all the time. He'd lie for self-aggrandizing reasons, or for some other advantage, social or professional, and he'd lie for absolutely no reason at all. Then he'd say something that I was sure was a lie, and it would turn out to be true. It was enough to send you screaming through the wards.

"Oh, but sweetheart, it's harmless," Kitty would say when I complained. "He doesn't hurt anybody, does he?"

But he did. Keppel loved to gossip. To gossip about the great and the near-great was to show his intimacy with them, to let you know that he was inside, knew their secrets. Often his gossip was a lie, sometimes innocuous, sometimes malicious, as when he told a story about a colleague whose new, widely reviewed book was, according to Keppel, plagiarized from someone else's work. What Keppel said got around, and the author of the book publicly and convincingly and angrily refuted the rumor.

"John Smith is furious at you! He heard that you're the one who said his work was plagiarized from Tom Jones. Why in God's name did you say that when you knew it wasn't true?"

"I never said that," Keppel said serenely.

"I heard you!" I expostulated.

Keppel's teaching schedule was very light, as befits a celebrated academic—maybe one seminar a week given to six elite postdoctoral students. The rest of the time he wrote monographs for scholarly journals and gave lectures that he delivered in great halls in various cities. He also arranged for important European intellectuals to come to New York, where he entertained them lavishly on his university funds. In return, they were expected to lecture and to participate in panel discussions organized by Keppel: discussions on culture and architecture, culture and politics, culture and sexual deviance, culture and class, culture and language. The culture part was American culture, which always came in for a drubbing from the Europeans. Keppel identified with Europeans. Sometimes he lost his English and had to search for it in French: *"Comment dit-on . . . ?"*

I went to some of these lectures. You're already aware that I am not an esteemed intellectual, a celebrated theorist, or even a lowly adjunct instructor. So what did I know? But I was quite struck to find that Keppel's personal anecdotes and ruminations were material for rigorous intellectual discourse.

"You know," Keppel said to a packed audience one evening, "I was walking up Broadway the other day when it struck me that there is a distinct relation between street signs as signifiers, and sexual self-esteem."

If those were not his exact words, I promise you they're not far off.

Keppel told me he was going to Paris to have discourse with his idol, Michel Foucault. I may have misunderstood him, because when Keppel returned, he began to casually mention around town that he had been Foucault's lover. Did he say "discourse" or "intercourse"? Who knew? The man would say anything. And that brings us to another matter.

It was true, as Kitty had said, that Keppel was separated from his wife when she introduced us. But was what I had heard true—that he was gay? The answer is that sometimes he was gay and sometimes he wasn't; it depended on the occasion. "We gay men and women," he once said to an audience composed of gay men and women.

"Keppel," I said, "do you like boys better than girls?"

He was indignant. "*Comment dit-on? . . . Non,* of course not." Which meant, I guess, that he liked girls better. "But," he said, and his eyes went soft and dreamy, "sometimes when you travel, you meet a beautiful boy, and you have a night out of time."

Very poetic.

A few months later, the world learned that Foucault was very ill. Soon Foucault died. This was the time when gay men were dying of a mysterious illness. It had no name, and it didn't occur to me that Keppel might have this illness, although he certainly complained enough about ill health. But a few months later, I decided I'd had enough of Keppel. The lying, the amorphousness of his nature, and my own fear of developing high blood pressure, or even a stroke, from constant expostulation. I was tired of trying to pin Keppel down. To say nothing of the sex business, of which I will say nothing. You must be wondering why I hung around so long.

The long and the short of it is, I had been in it for what I could get. Not for the jewels with which Keppel might cover me; no, I wanted him to lead me into the world of acknowledged intellectuals, to meet the great and the near-great, to see if I could hold my own among them. I had gotten about as much as I could get out of Keppel. I said goodbye. He took it very well. Actually, he hardly seemed to notice.

And then, a few weeks later, came the dead-of-night telephone call. After I'd yelled, "Goddammit, Keppel," I hung up the phone. I went to the window. Sleet was hitting the window-pane. It was three o'clock in the morning. There were no taxis on the Bowery. I called my friend Michael, who lived a few blocks away. He sounded very grumpy.

"Michael, Michael, I'm so sorry, but you've got to get your car and pick me up." I told him what had happened.

Michael knew Keppel. "Oh, please. He's putting you on," he said. But he knew we had to go. On the way over in the car, I was thinking, Gosh, suppose it's true. Suppose Keppel has killed himself and left me everything. It was not a displeasing thought.

"Should we call the police?" I asked Michael. "Should we call 911?"

"Just wait until we get over there," Michael said. "I think you'll find we won't have to call anyone."

We rang Keppel's bell. We heard sounds from inside. Michael rolled his eyes. Someone fumbled with the lock. Keppel opened the door. He looked bleary-eyed, drunk. We went inside. I glanced at the typewriter. Nothing.

"Keppel," I said, "are you all right?"

"I'm fine," he said. "I was at a party. I just fell asleep."

"Why did you call me?" I said.

"Yeah, why did you call her?" Michael said.

"I didn't call you," Keppel said serenely.

I should mention that by this time the world had learned the name of the disease that killed Foucault.

"Keppel," I said very gently, "I came because I was wor-ried about you. You know, because of you and Foucault. Did you call me because you're afraid you have AIDS?" Just for the hell of it, I added, "Tell me the truth, Keppel."

Keppel's eyes widened. It never occurred to him that his

stories might have an afterlife. He'd almost forgotten the Foucault story, but now it was coming back to him. He was thinking about it, seeing how the story could play out, how his connection with Foucault might be engraved in history. Oh, he liked this idea!

"Yes," he said. "I went to the doctor today. He did some tests. I'll know the results in a few weeks."

Keppel smiled what he meant to be a brave smile. He was as serene as ever.

Stay

Our dog Harry briefly enjoyed a show-business career. Well, we enjoyed it. If Harry had a notion of celebrity, it had to do with food.

Harry's role, which was in a music video, was arranged by Phyllis, who was his trainer and walker, and who was also walker to a few dogs of the stars (Mary Tyler Moore's, Andie MacDowell's, Paul Simon's). Phyllis recommended Harry to play the part of Paul Simon's dog in a new song that mentioned a dog. We were thrilled but puzzled. First of all, why didn't Paul Simon use his own dog? If his dog wouldn't do, why not find one who more closely resembled the lyrics of his song, which called for a little dog? Harry was clearly medium-sized and weighed a muscular fifty-five pounds. More to the point, Harry was not reliable in the obedience department, as Phyllis had good reason to know.

The video actually got made. We saw a tape of it. And

since it is more than unlikely that you will ever see it, I'll describe it.

Simon's song is rather high-toned: it's about the French artist René Magritte and his wife, Georgette, who sought refuge in New York during World War II. In the video, we see the Magrittes, played by Paul Simon and his then-wife, Carrie Fisher, strolling arm in arm through Central Park, wearing clothes to evoke the forties: a bowler hat for Paul, a knee-length, chunky fur coat thrown over Carrie's shoulders. Their dog is at their heels and, as they stroll, we hear the song, which includes the phrase *"Mr. and Mrs. Magritte and their little dog after the war . . ."*

Paul and Carrie are more or less dressed for the part, but the hulking, shaggy black-and-white terrier mutt behind them must have escaped from another song. It is ludicrously obvious that the only reason Harry has agreed to follow these people is that in Paul Simon's free hand, which dangles by his side, there is a large biscuit. You can see the biscuit, which is just out of Harry's reach, and you can see that Harry is almost on tiptoe, straining his neck to the utmost, trying to get at it. Verisimilitude is shattered: this dog does not belong to that couple. In any case, the song never made the charts, and the video was the beginning and end of Harry's career, although we still speak of it, as we still speak of Harry.

From our courtship days, Ben spoke to me of dogs. Airedales were frequently mentioned.

"An Airedale, for instance. So companionable. He'd lie at your feet, his head on his paws, his eyes adoring you . . ."

I'd had a few dogs in my time, so I knew that passive adoration was only part of the picture. But I made the amateur debater's classic mistake by accepting my opponent's terms of argument.

"Airedales," I said, "cost hundreds of dollars. That's immoral when the shelters are filled with abandoned dogs."

"True!" Ben said happily. "So you agree, definitely a terrier."

Here's a riddle: when is an Airedale a red herring?

When we weren't talking about dogs, we talked about getting married. There was a small problem.

"Let's be sensible about this," Ben said. "We'll consult with Dr. Bruin."

Dr. Bruin was Ben's neurologist. The problem was that Ben had multiple sclerosis. His symptoms were still mild. Mildish. Trouble walking. Some days he could walk with two canes, some days he had to use a scooter. He could drive a car with hand controls, he could cook dinner, he could do a number of other things you might imagine a woman would appreciate.

Let's suppose for a moment that Dr. Bruin had spoken straightforwardly about the disease. In that case, he would have told us that the course of MS is unpredictable. He would have mentioned the possibility of Ben's paralysis progressing inexorably. "Spasms" is another word he would have used. He would have told us about bodily functions—loss of control thereof. What would we have done in that case?

No doubt exactly what we did, because we were in love. We would have said to each other: "But he said it *might* happen, that doesn't mean it *will* happen. And even if it should happen, we'll manage." Or that's what I would have said.

As it did happen, Dr. Bruin said none of the above. He said the opposite. He leaned forward in his chair, he put his elbows on his desk, he went puff-puff on his pipe, he looked us in the eye. Eyes. "In my opinion," he said in his deeply reassuring European accent, "the disease has burned itself out. It will not progress further."

Wow! Burned out. No further progression. We were so happy we got married right away.

"Let's call him Philip," Ben said.

"*Philip?* Here, *Philip?* Sit, *Philip?*"

"Harry?"

We were lying in bed watching Philip, or Harry, chase his too-long tail.

Yes. He was Harry. And this was a Sunday morning in the cold spring of 1981. We were in northern Massachusetts, where we had gone to visit friends. The dog question had been decided: the person who wants something more than the person who doesn't want it wins. Anyway, it had rained all of Saturday. What was there to do in the country on a rainy day? We checked the local paper for inspiration. At Ben's suggestion, we read the classifieds. So many ads offering puppies! For example: "Adorable black-and-white puppy for adoption."

Our hostess and I took a drive. In an hour or so, we had exhausted the puppy population in the environs of Amherst; dozens of short-haired, brown, houndish mutts yipped and scrambled around muddy yards. Then we drove to a town called Florence, where we inspected the adorable black-and-white puppy. He was indoors, which gave him the advantage of cleanliness. His mother happened to be at home. I must say, she was the oddest-looking dog I ever saw, with a big brown wiry head on a sausage-shaped, short-legged body. Harry did not resemble her in the least. He was mostly black, with a white muzzle, white chest and paws, and white on the tip of his tail; he had rough, shaggy fur that made a fringe over his eyes. Definitely some kind of terrier mix. Three months old, and already he'd been touched by tragedy: someone had adopted him, kept him for a week, and returned him. Poor little puppy. He let me pet him, he wagged his tail and licked my hand. I melted. "He's the one," I said, and didn't think to ask why he'd been returned.

The sweet puppy who slept on my lap during the long drive home was a wild dog. He wouldn't sit and he wouldn't stay. He tore up cushions, he gnawed on books. If I came between him and his food, he growled at me. The aggressive little monster picked dogfights and worked himself into a killing rage. We had him fixed, which helped, but he had to be locked away when infants and small children appeared. I'm sure he thought of them as vermin, because terriers, as I learned too late, are bred specifically to destroy vermin around the farm. They are bred to do this job as independent agents, without reference to human instruction.

We needed help, and that was when we found Phyllis, who trained Harry to sit and stay so well that he became the demo dog in her training classes. When she brought him back to us, he was the same old Harry. This was sometimes humiliating, as when Phyllis brought him home from a training class when we had guests.

"Harry, sit!" I said, wanting to show him off. Nothing.

Sometimes I loved Harry, sometimes I hated him.

When I loved him, I called him pet names, such as Roddy

McDowall, not because I foresaw his eventual show-business connection but because of his eyes, which were just like Roddy McDowall's big, brown human eyes behind the ape mask in *Planet of the Apes*. Sometimes I murmured to Harry, "Are you my beastly boy?" This was love too. When I hated him, I called him "this dog."

"This dog is a nightmare," I'd say to Ben. "He's ruining my life." Honestly? Sometimes I wasn't sure if it was Harry I meant.

Pace Dr. Bruin, in time we were forced to seek other medical opinions. "Burned out?" said Dr. Smith. "Who ever told you such a thing?" This was not a disease that burned out. If you were lucky, you could live a lifetime with mild symptoms—oh, you might become fatigued easily; you might experience temporary periods of weakness in your legs or arms; your vision might grow blurred from time to time.

Ben got unlucky, we got unlucky. This disease was a slow train on a one-way track, traveling from the soles of Ben's feet to the tops of his shoulders. First it finished the job on his legs; it rested for a while at his midsection, the better to do a thorough job deactivating organ reflexes; then it moved up to disable his arms.

If you can believe it, things might have been worse: MS could have paralyzed Ben's swallowing reflex, and that would have been curtains; if it had paralyzed the breathing muscles of his diaphragm, that would have been curtains too. Best of all, it spared his brain, although we neglected to give thanks for such favors. After ten years, the facts on the ground, as far as Ben was concerned, were: no more walking, no more going to the movies on impulse, no more writing by hand or typewriter, goodbye to the pleasures of solitary reading, never again to turn over in bed—just for the sake of turning, mind you, not necessarily to put his arms around me.

As for me, I was in a state of panic during the early years, as each new symptom appeared and we had to learn how to manage it. Not only the symptom but the complications: infected bedsores, bacterial blood infections. Just as I thought we had things under control, something else went haywire, and we had to learn how to deal with that too. I had to learn to deal with it. Do you wonder that I thought of running away from home? Would you believe me if I said those were good years too?

And Harry? Bad dog that he was, he became our bad dog; no question that we belonged to him, and he to us. He was such an entertaining creature. When we took him to Riverside Park, he immediately looked around for a soccer game. If one was in progress, he made himself one of the boys. As soon as the ball was in play, he went after it, took it in his forepaws, ran with it, pushing it ahead of him through the south meadow while a half-dozen teenagers chased after him. If there was no soccer game, he'd insert himself into a game of Frisbee. The blimp was his enemy. He heard the motor long before it appeared and menaced the empty sky with his growls. "Uh-oh, a blimp must be coming," we'd say, and as soon as it hovered into sight Harry barked it off. He was a stalker of squirrels, with such a balletic and patient style that the most infirm squirrel could complete his business without hurry before Harry made the rush. Nothing frightened Harry except those toy cars that work by remote control; it must have been the sound of the electronic device, pitched too high for us to hear, that made him put his tail between his legs and run in the opposite direction.

If Ben's life had been filled with dogs, and it surely had been—Corky, Roderick, Chaing, Poppae, Burnham, Root—Harry was the dog of his life. No wonder. That weekend when we drove to Massachusetts and came home with Harry was the last time Ben would ever drive, and Harry was the last dog he would ever walk.

Phyllis took Harry for his early-morning walk. I walked him the rest of the time. Theoretically, he needed only two more walks a day, but very frequently he had diarrhea and dragged me to the park at two or three in the morning. For years the vet treated him for worms; finally, a new vet diagnosed inflammatory bowel disease. But by that time the disease had advanced too far, and treatment did little good. When he was eleven years old, Harry got cancer of the spleen. Just like him to pick such a bad time. My mother and father were in the last stages of their lives, falling down and breaking bones, in and out of hospitals. It seemed that every other day I was rushing sixty miles upstate for one emergency or another.

We had Harry's spleen taken out. After he recovered from the operation, he seemed fine. We were so happy. I ran into the vet in the park one afternoon. "Look at him!" I said. "He's himself again."

"Yes," said the vet. "That's good." She looked at Harry with no expression.

And soon Harry wasn't his old self. He didn't eat. He dragged himself from room to room. At night, on his pillow beside Ben's bed, he whimpered, and Ben tried to talk him through the night. In the afternoon, when I came home, he could barely wag his tail.

My father died one day in early March. This was 1992. A week later, I was upstate with my mother when Ben called.

"Harry's hemorrhaging," he said. "Phyllis is taking him to the vet."

An hour later, Ben called again. "They want to put him down." He was crying.

Phyllis called. "Should I let them?"

I called Ben. "Should we let them?"

"We have to," he said. "Oh my God, I wish I could be with him."

I wished Ben could be with me.

It wasn't too many months later that my mother died. I missed her by two hours.

Wasn't that a bad time?

For months and months afterward, I dreamed about my mother every night, and Ben dreamed about Harry. One afternoon when he woke up from a nap, he told me he'd dreamed a poem. I wrote it down:

I was a bad dog and didn't obey
any command, until today.

He dreamed the title too. "Stay."

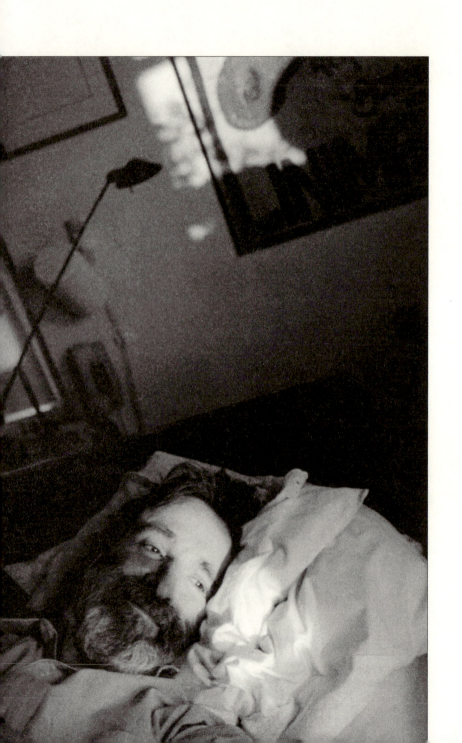

Strangers in the House

You simply can't get good help anymore.

I say this as a woman required to do so. Not that I was raised for such: never in her life did my mother have so much as a weekly cleaning lady, and this was a matter of principle as much as money. For me, in my previous life, it was money, although during a briefly prosperous period, I hired a woman named Divine Love. Later, I married into illness, for which help is a necessity if you're lucky enough to afford it.

In our early days, our honeymoon days, we had Bertha. Bertha came five days a week to do the housework and look after Ben. Ben's MS wasn't very advanced. He could do pretty much everything. He walked, he typed, he cooked, he made love. But his legs weren't working so well. Sometimes he fell. One day, pumped up on steroids, he ran down the subway steps and broke a leg. He began to use a cane, then two canes, a walker. Eventually,

he sat down on a little scooter, and after that he didn't get up anymore.

At some point I noticed that Bertha was drinking. When
she was drunk, she muttered darkly.

"Bertha," I'd say, "you're drunk."

"Not drunk!"

"Bertha, I smell it!"

"Jess a lil' beer to relax me," she'd say. And then she'd
telephone my friend Jenny to complain about being abused
by me.

"Bertha," I said, "I think it's time for you to retire." We
gave Bertha a huge amount of money and Linda came to keep
the house. A year or two after that, Ben's arms became useless.
That was the big change, because then he needed more help than
I could give. So we hired Alva, and for weekends Ninetta.

I will say nothing here of various transitory helpers: of
Lola, who threatened to bash me with an uplifted chair; of
Pauline, who borrowed $1,500 on the strength of an eviction
notice and immediately disappeared. No, our essential and stable
cast for a long time was Linda, who came to clean the house and
do laundry a couple of days a week; Alva, who lived with us on
weekdays to take care of Ben; and Ninetta, who took Alva's place
on weekends.

One day in 1991, B arrived for a job interview with Ben.
(Our lawyer says I should not name her, but I feel somehow
compelled to reveal that her real name is A.) When B entered our
apartment, this was what she saw: in a large, sunny room—our
living room—a darkly handsome man, his beard streaked with
white, seated in a large electronic wheelchair. Ben did not rise at
B's entrance, he did not extend his hand, so B would have

quickly gathered that he was paralyzed except for his head and shoulders.

Ben would have seen a young woman. Slim, blond, angular. Not a beauty. (Her mouth was too thin, her eyes were too close-set, her long chin had a definite upward curve.) But she was attractive enough, crisp and clean: her hair was glossy, her clothes pressed, her pale skin without blemish. In her soft voice (I give her that, in the interest of complete disclosure), she would have told Ben that she had literary interests. This would have been important, since she was speaking to a published author and an editor who had founded a celebrated literary magazine. But B's real ambition was to make documentary films. She would not have stressed the fact that she had not yet made any, and that, as she was thirty-three and time was getting on, this was a little worrying.

The job on offer was to come to our house for four hours every weekday, to take Ben's dictation on the computer, to keep the office in order, to be generally pleasant and helpful. B was not exactly in the category of domestic help: her status in the household was more that of a governess than of an upstairs maid. But she was help, and she was in the house.

There is always a first time—the first cigarette before it becomes a habit, the first murder before it becomes thrillingly serial. I'm not sure of the date, but all the evidence indicates that the first time B stole money from Ben was early in 1994. That means Ben had had three years to develop trust in B. To see himself as her mentor, a role he relishes, particularly with young women. And perhaps this time it was something more. I'm sure that B knew exactly how Ben felt. I suspect she may have had a slightly different view of their relationship.

Let's say that on a day in 1994, B looked in her wallet and realized that she was low on cash. But perhaps she already had a plan, and with the plan a theory to justify it. That interests me. Among college-educated middle-class girls, wanting money isn't justification enough for stealing it. It needs rationalization. What was B's?

At that moment in 1994, B finds herself alone in the office. Very casually, she gets up from her desk and strolls down the short corridor leading to the bedroom. So far, there is no one in sight. She makes a left turn into a bright, pleasant room. The walls are crowded with pictures and books, the windows face south to the Hudson. There is a hospital bed, but also some nice furniture, including a pretty red-painted bureau centered on the west wall of the bedroom. As B well knows, Ben's wallet is in the top drawer of the bureau. She opens the bureau drawer, takes out the wallet, and removes some cash. (How much was it that first time?) She slips the money into the back pocket of her jeans and strolls from the room.

But here's a stunner! When B enters the bedroom, she sees Linda, making the bed. Surely at that moment B is startled. Wouldn't you, wouldn't I, turn back? Say something like "Oh. Linda. I was just looking for Ben's glasses." But as we have seen, that didn't happen. And as it turns out, B's gamble pays off. Linda sees B take the money, and she says nothing, not to B, not to Ben, not to me.

Why not? Much later, I asked Linda this question. Her answer was something to the effect of: "I'm just the housekeeper from the jungles of Brazil. B is a white girl, the boss's secretary; he must have said it was okay to take the money. Anyway, I'm not going to make trouble; I could lose my job." And B, who was otherwise so vocal in her sympathies with the peoples of the developing world, so strictly politically correct, depended for her protection on this class difference. Or so I imagine.

Let's give B the benefit of the doubt this one time: let's say that on this occasion, she was repaying herself for an item she had bought for Ben.

But cash continues to inexplicably disappear. Ben says to B, "I know I had more money in my wallet. And what's happening to the office cash?"

B shrugs. I wonder: is there a veiled suggestion in that shrug, and perhaps in a raised eyebrow? Does she intend Ben to infer that Linda is taking it, that Alva is taking it, that I am taking it?

"Well, let's stash it in a book," says my husband.

Without batting an eye, cool as a cucumber, butter wouldn't melt in her mouth, B chooses the book—a volume of art history, I believe—in which to hide the cash. And still cash is disappearing. Wouldn't you think the man would get a glimmer?

But no. Ben, a man of enthusiasms, is B's enthusiast. "How intelligent B is," my husband tells me, "how varied and deep her interests; this film she wants to make, I'd like to help her." At some point he begins to refer to B as his partner.

Do you see what's going on here? Because I didn't.

As for Linda, she may not have told us what she saw in the bedroom that day, but she has told Alva. They're from the same country, they speak the same language, they're friends; of course she told Alva. What wonderful gossip! What human interest! And power! They know something we don't know. From now on they keep their eyes open and notice how often a certain large red volume of art history is taken from the shelf.

"B, could you come in here?" Linda hears Ben call from the living room.

"I'll be right there," B replies, and Alva or Linda watch as B coolly replaces a big red book on the shelf and sticks some cash into her knapsack.

Alva is a strange one. A tiny woman, probably in her late thirties when she came to us. Cute: like a cross between a cat and a lemur. I spent weeks teaching her how to take care of Ben. To wash him, dress him, get him up from bed with the mechanical lift, help him into his chair.

At first she has no English at all, and I mistake her silence for serenity. As she learns the language, she turns into a chatterer. She intimates that she once had a husband—or is it a lover?—who did her wrong. Somebody did her wrong. She hints that once upon a time, wealth was her portion, and a grander style of life. I sense bitterness and volatility: she professes love for me, for Ben, but after a while she loves only our dog, Daisy.

Oh, how she loves our little black Daisy!

"Daisy is my happiness," she tells me. "You believe?"

"I believe."

And then she tells me about the trustworthiness of animals in contrast to the people who have dared to cross her. All those people—they lived to regret the advantage they took of Alva: she has taken her revenge on them.

This is all a bit worrying to me. But Alva is so competent, she takes such good care of Ben, that I want her to stay. To tell the truth, I don't want to take the time and trouble to train someone else. So I listen to all her stories, I offer advice, I soothe her, I agree with her. I can't seem to achieve the civil but distant manner appropriate to an employer. Friendliness, or its appearance, is the best I can do.

Inevitably, one day about five years into our "friendship," Alva turns on me.

What did I do? What did I say? Did I make the mistake of praising Ninetta, who is her weekend rival? Did I inadvertently miscount her salary and leave out a twenty-dollar bill?

It starts one evening after dinner. We are in the kitchen, loading the dishwasher.

"You think I love you," Alva says. "You think everybody loves you. Nobody likes you. They talk about you behind your back. They tell me what they really think."

What is she talking about? Why is she yelling at me? And who are these people telling her what they really think of me? Linda? Ninetta? B? Come to think of it, I have noticed a certain coziness between Alva and B: much tea drinking in the kitchen, Alva chattering, B listening.

For a month Alva heaps angry contempt on me. Sometimes I feel I've been hijacked into that movie where Dirk Bogarde reduces his employer to sniveling slavery. At last I've had enough. One day I say, "Alva, I don't want to come home every day to someone who hates me. You have to leave." I give her four weeks' notice.

Ninetta, who has been working weekends, will take Alva's weekday job. Alva has trained her, and she is a little frightened of Alva, as I now am myself. Still, they have become friendly enough so that Alva has confided in Ninetta what she and Linda know. Now three of our employees are keeping B's secret. Four, if you count B.

But Ninetta hates B. As she sees it, B not only usurps Ben's affections, which rightfully should be hers, but she gets his money. B works, what? Four hours a day, and most of the time she comes late. She sweet-talks Ben, then rolls her eyes behind his back. She spends hours on the phone with her friends. She leaves her used cups and dishes around the house for someone else to pick up.

This is intolerable to Ninetta, who works her ass off. Ninetta is as fierce as a pit bull, or a Sicilian on a quest for *giustizia*.

"You know what goes on in this house, Dorothy," Ninetta says to me. It's not a question.

"What do you mean, Ninetta?"

"You know. You know."

No, how would I know? No one tells me anything. Cryptic hints in pidgin English are all I get.

Ninetta watches B constantly. She's on her like white on rice. Ninetta notes the pilfering of cash, but she's noticed something else. The checkbook.

"You think you are queen in this house," Ninetta says to me. "You are not the queen."

"Who is queen, Ninetta? You?"

"No, I am not. You know who is."

No. I know nothing. But I must say that something is making me uneasy.

"Ben," I say, "Linda says she doesn't work for B. So please ask B to put her leftover food in the garbage and her dishes in the dishwasher."

"Ben," I say, "the office is a mess. Books and papers are piling up on every surface. Why isn't B filing this stuff?"

"Ben," I say, "B always comes late. It interferes with everyone's routine."

Mind you, I am not at home during most of B's tour, but when I come home, I notice that she is always talking and laughing softly into the phone, clearly not on Ben's business. I notice that she reads magazines in the pauses between Ben's dictation, and that she seems irritated when he begins to dictate again. And here's something that really riles me: when B uses the last of the toilet paper in my bathroom, she doesn't replace it. Not just once does she neglect to replace it, not just twice. She *never* replaces it! How often have I reached back to find an empty cardboard roll? It's a small thing, right? But when it's a regular thing, rather aggressive in a passive way, no?

"Ben," I say, "please ask her to replace the toilet paper, do the filing, clean up her messes."

Ben says, "We're working on a documentary. I'm going to produce it."

Well. You tell me what it means to be a producer. My understanding is that it means providing the money.

"Are you giving B the money for this movie?"

"Some of it," he says.

I suspect that he is underreporting.

This is a facer.

And by what right do I interfere?

Because you could drown in Ben's needs, and I am trying to stay afloat. Can you imagine how enormous his needs are, how engulfing? His mind is whole, and he needs the whole of life—friends, work, travel, movies, love, sex. For nine years he ran a literary magazine (with a staff of beautiful girls, I might add; none stole a penny, though I suspect that one or two briefly stole his heart). He wrote a brilliant memoir, but now his energy is sinking, and although he still writes, the pieces are short and take a long time to complete. Once a passionate reader, he can no longer turn the pages of a book; once a world traveler, he now has trouble getting on a local bus. Not to speak of turning on a light switch or turning on the television set, making a phone call, rolling over in bed, feeding himself.

In the years before total paralysis set in, we were almost like normal people. We drove to Massachusetts to stay with friends; we flew to Colorado for Ben's daughter's graduation; we rented a house on Long Island for a few weeks; we went to the movies and the theater, restaurants.

We couldn't keep it up, not without an entourage of help that we couldn't afford. With the increasing paralysis, the bladder and bowel problems, and the spasms that came with it all, I began to say, "No, we can't go, it's too hard for me." We still laughed a lot, but all forms of physical fun went out the window.

So that was where we were when B came along. My husband, his life increasingly locked in, and every day when I am off working, B is offering Ben a life. Sometimes they go to movies together, to museums. Incidentally, doesn't he love films? Why not underwrite her project? To what extent? To the extent of the budget she presents to him. Is the budget inflated? I'd bet the house on it! In return for all this money, in return for access to Ben's friends who can help her, Ben gets B's companionship and a big credit as producer. In this way, thousands of dollars are transferred to B. Legitimately. And, by the way, Ben is happy.

I didn't interfere. I had no right.

STRANGERS IN THE HOUSE • 113

• • •

"So, Alva," I say cheerfully. "This is your last day with us."

Alva screams. She falls to the floor, writhing. Her arms and legs jerk and flail. A seizure? I call for B and hold Alva's jerking arms while B forces a spoon into her mouth. B is bending over Alva, and I am calling 911, when I hear Alva whisper to B, "Don't leave me alone with Dorothy, she'll kill me."

The EMS technician takes a look at the "fit" and puts a bag over Alva's face: hyperventilation. She has worked herself into this state. Nevertheless, they take her to the emergency room. I cannot leave Ben; B goes with her. That night Ben says to me, "You ought to talk to B. Tell her about your troubles with Alva."

"B," I say the next day, "I'm really grateful that you took Alva to the hospital. I'd like to tell you why I fired her."

B is sitting at her desk reading. She doesn't look up. "I don't want to hear it," she says.

Now *this* is odd. Hostile, actually. I think about all those times I reached for the toilet paper to find an empty roll. I think about the cozy tea parties in the kitchen, B and Alva chatting away. All those hours B has spent with Alva, no doubt listening to tales of my egregious nature.

"B was distinctly unfriendly to me," I say to Ben. "I'm taking offense. You should too."

How could I have imagined the next step in this drama?

"Alva is going to sue you," Linda says to me.

"What for?"

"She's going to say that she hurt her wrist working here. Also that you were paying her off the books."

"Oh, please," I say. "She's got no case."

"Listen to me," Linda says. "B is helping her."

"What do you mean?"

"Just believe me. Don't say anything in front of B that you don't want Alva to know. B will tell her. B went with Alva to a lawyer to give a deposition against you."

"I don't believe it."

"I'm telling you. Also, Alva asked me to kidnap Daisy."

What is going on here? Just in case Linda is not paranoid, I write out a long statement to our lawyer. I describe Alva's five years of employment with us and the reasons I fired her. I fax the statement. Stupidly, stupidly, because I cannot fathom such betrayal, I leave the original statement next to the fax machine. The next day, when I look for it, it's gone.

"That paper you sent to your lawyer?" Linda says. "B took it. She gave it to Alva. Alva gave it to her lawyer."

I tell Ben. He doesn't believe it, I can't believe it, we ignore it. B continues her work as usual. And remember: we still don't know about the money. And even if we had known, we wouldn't have known the half of it.

What I think now is that B's relationship with Alva was, in part, an alliance of necessity on B's part. Alva knew about the money. But B was also a girl who liked to be in the right: to hold correct political and moral positions. The badly mistreated third-world Alva—exploited and abused, as she would have insisted—must have been balm to B's conscience. Yes, wasn't she, B, making a political statement by exploiting the exploiter? Even apart from that, Ben was so generous, he cared so much for B, wouldn't he have wanted her to have what she needed?

But really, I'm grasping at straws here.

• • •

Now it's 1999. One evening Ninetta says, "Dorothy, come to the kitchen. I want to show you something."

We sit at the kitchen table. Ninetta hands me the office checkbook. "Look. Count. How many times she pays herself her salary?"

B has had free access to the office checkbook: she pays the office bills. She affixes Ben's signature with the stamp authorized by the bank. She writes the checks for her salary.

The checkbook Ninetta gives me goes back only one year. I begin to count. How many weeks were there last year? Seventy-two? Because that's how many salary checks B wrote to herself. Instead of four checks a month, there are often six, each made out for the exact amount of her salary. And when her two-week vacation rolls around, she pays herself for four weeks.

A checkbook is like a novel. I read in it the day B's salary was raised by $100 a week. That was a year earlier.

In 1998, B asked Ben for a raise. A hundred dollars a week, please.

"You know I can't afford that," Ben said. "I have to cut expenses; money is just pouring out. I don't understand it. At this rate, I won't have enough to go on working very much longer."

B burst into tears.

"I'll give you fifty," Ben said.

And still B wept. Really she did, as though she had forgotten that her tricks with the checkbook and the wallet had already raised her salary by quite a bit, perhaps by enough so that she and her boyfriend could afford the lovely new apartment they moved into. She had been embezzling for so long without being caught that she may have believed she was entitled to every check she wrote to herself. So just last year, with Ben, she wept and sincerely pleaded for her well-deserved raise until he gave in.

As she continued to write her own checks for her salary, each one included her $100 raise, as did each of the unauthorized salary checks. Nothing fancy about her method of embezzlement; it was simple and effective as long as no one was counting.

I went to the basement where the canceled checks were stored. I rooted through everything in that dusty, dirty storeroom. I took it all to the accountant.

"Anything amiss here?" I asked the accountant, who had not been counting either.

So, over a five-year period starting in 1994, B wrote herself checks amounting to about $40,000 above her salary. We'll never know how much cash she took. And this was in addition to the thousands Ben voluntarily handed over for her art's sake. What this amount signifies—no secret to B, who knew exactly the condition of Ben's finances—is that there will come a time, two or three years earlier than it should have, when Ben can no longer afford to pay an assistant, and therefore, when he can no longer write, no longer keep up correspondence, he will no longer keep a place in the world.

Ben is devastated, humiliated, heartbroken. He telephones B. "Is this true?" he asks.

B bursts into tears. "Oh," she sobs, "I'm so bad with money."

Well put, wouldn't you say?

• • •

Oh my goodness, the themes you stumble over as you make your way from day to day! Trust, Betrayal, Class, Hypocrisy, Love, Hate, Greed, Sickness, Health. It only needs War and Peace.

Somewhere in all this, there must be a lesson. Is it: don't get cozy with the help? Is it that household politics are simply politics writ small? Is it that greed and betrayal lurk like bacteria awaiting a failure of the immune system? Is it that one should always use a bonded employment agency? Is it life, or what?

Dumb Luck

What . . .
If I'd been born
in the wrong tribe,
with all roads closed before me?

— WISLAWA SZYMBORSKA

Liya Alexandrovna Gordeeva is my first cousin once removed. Some people are confused by the once-removed relationship, but it's really very simple. The removal takes place parallel with generations: the child of my mother's sister (or brother) is my first cousin; the child of this first cousin is my first cousin once removed; if my once-removed cousin should have a child, it will be my first cousin twice removed. I won't get into the second- and third-cousin business.

I could simply have said that Liya Alexandrovna is my

cousin and let it go at that, but I wanted to make the point that Liya is not a close relative. Not only that, she was born in Moscow and has never left that city. Until last summer, I had never been to Moscow and so had never laid eyes on her.

I did know that she existed. I knew that she was the daughter of my mother's niece, Betya. I knew that (things being what they were in the Soviet Union) my mother and her sisters had regularly sent money to Betya. I knew that Betya had a daughter named Liya and that the two of them had always lived together, much to Betya's dismay. When Betya died, which was sometime in the late eighties, my mother and her sisters continued to send money to Liya.

The long and the short of it is that the time came when my cousins and I inherited Liya. We took it for granted that we were obligated to send her money, as our mothers had done, and we knew that except for us, Liya was all alone: no husband, no children, no other relatives, no job. We had the impression that she somehow wasn't equipped to make her way in the world.

It didn't seem so onerous a burden to take responsibility for one person in the world among the millions in need. We chipped in; every third month, I wired three hundred dollars to Moscow and didn't think of Liya Alexandrovna until the next time this act of filial piety was due.

Things went on in this way for a number of years. We sent the money, Liya collected it. And then she didn't. A year's worth of money piled up in the Western Union office in Moscow. What to do? Maybe Liya had died. We located an agency that catered to Moscow's Jewish population, and pretty soon I got an e-mail from a social worker:

Dear Dorothy,

I visited your cousin Liya Alexandrovna Gordeeva in her apartment in Moscow on November 16, 2004. I was able to talk to Ms. Gordeeva and enter her apartment with the assistance of Liya's neighbor. Normally, Liya doesn't allow strangers into her apartment.

Liya looked unkempt, untidy (a torn housedress, uncombed hair, torn slippers, clearly in need of a bath). The apartment was stuffy and dusty. There is a broken bed in one of the rooms. There is a big crack along the kitchen wall. There are cockroaches in the kitchen. There is no refrigerator, no washer. Her phone has been disconnected for nonpayment.

Liya receives a pension of 2,383 roubles a month ($90). She pays 950 roubles for the utilities and apartment maintenance, and about 260 roubles for medications for her heart. She eats one meal a day. Typically she has oatmeal, or macaroni and tea. There's a grocery close by where she could go herself, but she doesn't go because she cannot afford anything. She said that her U.S. relatives used to send her money but she got sick and couldn't pick up the money transfers. When she finally got to the bank it was too late, and the bank refused to give it to her.

Liya refused any assistance or services. She says that she can clean the house herself, but she doesn't feel like doing so. She is also very frightened to go any distance from her apartment . . .

Oh. *This* was my once-removed cousin. Suddenly real in torn housecoat and slippers. I could see her shuffling around that apartment. I could see the cockroaches scuttling in the kitchen, the crack in the wall. I could feel the depression and loneliness that kept her from cleaning house. I could imagine that when she woke up every morning, a hot cup of tea was her only comfort in the long hours of nothing to do, no one to see, one paltry meal to mark the end of another day. I thought about the year Liya had been born, 1944, and what it meant to be born in Moscow during the war. I thought of Liya's mother, Betya, of Betya's mother, Rivka, who was my own mother's sister, and what it had meant to those three women to live their lives in that benighted country from which most of their family had the luck to escape.

On my way to Moscow last September, I stopped off in the Ukraine. Since I was going in that direction anyway, I wanted to take a look at my mother's hometown. The town is called Murafa, and it is a *very* small town, not even a dot on most maps. If, by some chance, you want to locate it, find Kiev on the map, then move your finger southwest about an inch, where you should find the city of Vinnitsya; continue on that line for less than an eighth of an inch. Unless you have a large-scale map, you won't find the name, Murafa, but that's where it is. Or, if you should ever find yourself in the town of Shargorod, drive past the statue of Lenin in the center of town, continue east on that road for seven kilometers, through hilly, wild countryside, then bear left after the hammer-and-sickle monument that to this day marks the road into Murafa.

The first thing you will see, should you drive into town, is a Roman Catholic cathedral, built by a Polish count in the eighteen hundreds; then an Orthodox church, both looming on the town's unpaved, dusty main street. My mother saw those churches every day, as well as the hilly green landscape and the houses, hidden for the most part down dirt lanes behind overgrown brush and tiny garden plots. I'd never seen such defiantly undecorated houses: no carved wood, no paint, no pleasure for the eye, each house an assertion that shelter is the best you can hope for.

Just a few steps from the town, the old Jewish cemetery still exists. It was vandalized during the war but, miraculously, not destroyed. Hundreds and hundreds of age-blackened head-stones, the oldest dated 1638, roll with the landscape across a grassy plateau that drops sharply away to fields below. The inscriptions on the stones are too faint to make out, even for someone who can read Hebrew, which I cannot. But the carvings are still distinct—a pair of praying hands indicates that a priestly Cohen is buried beneath; a bird in flight memorializes a woman named Faigle, which means "bird"; a water pitcher for a Levi. In one section of the cemetery, a grove of apple trees drop perfect fruit between the stones.

But at the center of town, where the open market was once held, where the Jewish houses clustered, where the Jewish shops were built, where Jewish trades were practiced, where three syn-agogues stood, nothing. A rubble-strewn space overgrown with weeds. Dead ground.

My grandfather kept a shop here. My grandmother, begin-ning her labors before the turn of the last century, gave birth to nine children here. One of her sons died of scarlet fever when he was five or six years old, and his bones probably lie in the Jew-ish cemetery. Of the other children, seven made it to America, where they lived long lives and died of nothing more serious than disease, one fluke accident, and old age. Only Rivka, the first of my grandmother's children, my mother's eldest sister, was left behind.

• • •

Rivka Rendar married Aron Vaks in Murafa. I have a picture taken on their wedding day. There are three people in the photograph. Rivka, seated on a bentwood chair in the photographer's studio, a pretty, pale girl, her face still rounded with baby fat. She is dressed in white. A ruffle is at her throat, a flounce decorates her sleeves, a locket is hung around her neck. I can just make out a white shoe beneath the hem of her dress. Her left elbow is propped on the tasseled arm of the chair, her chin rests on her hand. She leans toward her mother, my grandmother, who is seated next to her. It seems to me that my grandmother looks a little dispirited, considering the occasion, and neither is the bride smiling. Standing behind the two women is the new husband, Aron, a dark, thin, serious-looking boy wearing a three-piece suit, with a watch chain draped across his waistcoat.

I see that Rivka's hair is light, no doubt the same shade of reddish-blond that turns up in my family now and then. Her face is the original version of her sisters' faces, which are as familiar to me as my own. Aron seems delicate, definitely not robust. My grandmother may already suspect that he will not be a good earner, which may account for her grim expression.

The date of this marriage is not recorded, but I can make an educated guess. I figure that it is late 1913, or early the following year, because in 1915 Rivka will give birth to her daughter, Betya. I'm pretty sure that the wedding took place in Murafa, which is not only Rivka's hometown but probably Aron's as well. I say this because Vaks—Aron's family name—is written in the Murafa town register for the year 1945.

"Aren't there any earlier records?" I asked the mayor of Murafa.

"No," he said. "Everything was destroyed during the war."

I pointed to a word that followed all the Jewish names in the register. "What does this mean?"

"It means 'left,' " he said. "They all left."

I can tell you this much: the Ukrainian countryside is beautiful, and it reminds me of Iowa or Idaho. In mid-September, when the harvest is in, flocks of crows and geese settle on the rich black soil to glean the leavings. Murafa itself is as strange and otherworldly to me as those crossroads in the middle of the American nowhere that serve as towns for Indian reservations—a few shabby buildings in an empty countryside, under a dwarfing sky. I am helpless to imagine the life that was lived here. And is lived here still, except that there are no Jews anymore. I see that old women sit all day by the side of the road, minding a single cow as it grazes. As we drive through the country, I see that it is studded with plaques memorializing the massacres of World War II: BOW YOUR HEAD PASSERBY . . . At a railroad station, where freight cars stand on the sidings, a notice: FROM HERE 500,000 JEWS WERE SENT TO BERDICHEV . . . In Kiev, near the beautiful cathedral of Santa Sophia, I saw a huge monumental bronze statue of a man seated on a rearing horse.

Who is that? I ask. Why, that's Bohdan Khmelnytsky, a seventeenth-century hero of Ukrainian history. In his quest to liberate the Ukraine from Poles and their agents, the Jews, his Cossacks killed hundreds and thousands of them, impaling some alive on wooden stakes.

And one day, in Murafa, my aunt Rivka married a local boy, for love or not.

If we assume that the wedding took place early in the spring of 1914, we know that the sky was about to fall. In the space of a historical fraction of a second, World War I would come, the Bolshevik coup would follow, civil war would erupt; famine was around the corner. My grandfather was not so prescient, but he knew the present and the past. He knew that he lived in a place where Jews were an untouchable, despised caste. Almost everything had been forbidden to them: to move outside the Pale of Settlement, even to travel inside it without a permit; to own land, to go to school, except by minuscule quota. Jews were blamed for everything. For the assassination of Czar Alexander II. For the ritual murder of Christian children so as to obtain Christian blood to bake in their matzos.

"Nine-tenths of the troublemakers are Jews, and the people's whole anger turned against them . . . That's how the pogrom happened," Czar Nicholas wrote to his mother. He was referring to the six-hundred-odd pogroms that took place in the failed revolutionary year of 1905, when more than three thousand Jews were murdered. Once upon a time, it was common practice for Ukrainians to hang a Pole, a Jew, and a dog from the same tree. If this was a recreation peculiar to the seventeenth century, its spirit remained. You could never tell when the moment would come again.

In the early years of the twentieth century, Jews are leaving the country in droves, and my grandfather, too, has made his decision. One by one he is sending his children away. By the time Rivka married, three of his children, my mother included, were already in America. My grandfather intends the rest of the family to follow soon, and for our centuries-long sojourn in the Ukraine to come to an end.

Centuries-long? I don't know. There have been Jews in this part of the world for over a thousand years, wandering in from the east, the south, and the west as they were expelled elsewhere for the crime of being Jewish. Why, this place has hardly ever been a country at all. Its very name has been an invitation to hordes of murderous invaders: "Ukraine" means "no particular place," means "border-land." However long my family has lived here, it is long enough.

During World War I, half a million looting German and Austrian troops invaded the Ukraine. The war's end in 1918 scarcely made a difference. The Bolshevik coup brought ragtag Red and White armies, plus invading Poles, fighting a savage civil war, looting and raping their way through the towns and villages of the Ukraine. I don't have to imagine this. I need only open Isaac Babel's 1920 diary to the first entry. Here is Babel, riding with the Red Cavalry of Cossack troops. On June 3, they stop in the Ukrainian town of Zhitomir:

> *Zhitomir pogrom, organized by the Poles, continued, of course, by the Cossacks . . .*
>
> *Poles entered the town, stayed for 3 days, there was a pogrom, they cut off beards, that's usual, assembled 45 Jews in the marketplace, led to them to the slaughter yard, tortures, cut out tongues, wails heard all over the square. They set fire to 6 houses . . . machinegunned those who tried to rescue people. The yardman into whose arms a mother dropped a child from a burning building was bayoneted . . .*
>
> *The faces of the old Jews.*

On July 11:

Same old story, the Jews have been plundered, their
bewilderment, they expected the Soviet regime to liberate them
and suddenly there were shrieks, whips, cracking, shouts of
"dirty Yid."

One day a pogrom broke out in Murafa. Everyone fled the
house in panic, abandoning four-year-old Betya. I think of my
aunt Frieda, then fourteen or fifteen years old, who ran back to
get the baby.

I think of my grandfather's shop. What did he sell—dry
goods? Flour and salt? Syrups? His shop would have been
looted, all his stock confiscated. How did they survive, my
grandparents who had four young children at home, plus a married daughter, her husband, a grandchild? This would have been
the time to flee the country, but there was no getting out now:
the international borders were sealed.

I think it was in 1920 when my family, the Rendars,
together with Rivka and her family, the Vaks, left Murafa for a
town called Mogilev Podolski. They may have fled willy-nilly,
from fear and panic, and hunger, for famine swept the Ukraine
during the war years 1920–21. Here on my desk is another photograph of Rivka and her family taken in Mogilev, five or six
years after her wedding picture. She scarcely looks like the same
person. Hunger has sculpted her face, and she is all gaunt cheek-
bones and staring eyes. Aron is sunken in his chair, and most of
his hair is gone. Two children are with them now: Betya, five or
six years old, sullenly standing beside Rivka, with her hand in
her mother's lap. Aron holds their son, a boy, Yefim. The

woman standing behind them may be Aron's sister, and perhaps they fled to Mogilev because she offered to take them in.

But Mogilev may have been a more deliberate choice since it has the distinct advantage of being closer to an escape route. A moment came in the confusion of the civil war when my grandfather found a boatman willing to smuggle the family across the Dniester River into Moldova. From Moldova, they made their way to Bucharest, where the older girls, Frieda and Rachile, got factory jobs to support the family. Everyone waited—a year, even two—until the children in America could send for them. In the records of immigrants processed through Ellis Island, I find that Max and Chaika Rendar, together with four minor children—Frieda, Rachile, Iosif, and little Berka— were allowed to pass through the portals in 1922.

In fact, not all four children were minors: Frieda, who was twenty at the time, was passed off as seventeen, and Rachile as fifteen when she was actually eighteen. Rivka and Aron were long past such fudging. Two small children may have been sufficient reason to stay behind. Or maybe they said, "We'll join you later." But it occurs to me that Rivka may have consoled herself for the loss of her family with the Bolshevik promise of emancipation of the Jews. The new Soviet government had outlawed anti-Semitism. The Pale of Settlement had been lifted. Jews could move from their small shtetl towns to larger towns, to cities; they could be educated, join the professions. Jews were prominent in the new regime, they exercised power. In theory, Jews could become Soviets, if not actual Russians.

Rivka remained in close touch with her family after their emigration. Throughout the twenties, the families exchanged news.

Betya was going to school, and she seemed to have a talent for music. Yefim too had entered school, and Aron was as well as could be expected.

For her part, Rifka learned that American streets did not actually run with milk and honey, but little by little, her family was prospering. Her mother and father were still in good health; her sisters and brothers found work, and one by one they were getting married, children were being born: her favorite sister, Frieda, had a son. And everyone was eager for news of the Soviet Union. Was it true that Utopia was being created? A new Soviet Man? Indeed, Rachile, Rivka's youngest sister, was fervent in her belief that it was so. She had joined the American Communist Party, and she talked of returning to Russia.

And so she did. Rachile came in 1929. I suspect that she chose that time because an American delegation of the Communist Party of America was also traveling to Moscow then, to meet with the Comintern. Among the documents Rachile brought with her, and left with Rivka, was her membership card in the Communist Party, which shows that she had become a full-fledged member that year.

Political considerations aside, the reunion between the sisters was surely joyful. Almost a decade had passed since Rachile and Rivka had seen each other. Rachile was in her middle twenties, and a photograph taken at this time shows that she had become a strikingly beautiful woman. Rivka, in her mid-thirties, looks worn but lovely; the hungry look of the early twenties has disappeared. Betya, whom Rachile had taken care of as a small girl, was now a plump fourteen-year-old. Yefim, born after Rachile's emigration, was ten.

Evidently, nothing Rachile saw during her 1929 trip, nothing she heard during that decisive year when Stalin succeeded in ousting Trotsky from the leadership of the Party, discouraged her plan to make a permanent move. But by 1932, when she came back again, with her husband, Victor, planning to stay, events had taken a dreadful turn.

For Rachile, incredulity turned to disillusion. Disillusion went deep and was bitter and lifelong. Back in America, Rachile and Victor tried to describe what they had seen. My mother, for one, refused to believe them, and that rift between the sisters never healed. And what was it they had seen? Not your ordinary famine caused by war or a failure of the harvest. No, the Ukrainian harvest had been perfectly fine that year. This was Stalin's famine, his "revolution from above," the one that required breaking eggs for the omelet. The peasants of the Ukraine, so resistant to Stalin's plan for collectivization of farming, were to be crushed, starved, deported. It began with the requisition of food, all the food, all the seed stock. It proceeded to the point where one Party "activist," charged with the collection of foodstuffs in the Ukraine, wrote to his superior that he could meet the quota for meat, but it would have to be with human flesh. Boris Pasternak wrote, "What I saw could not be expressed in words. There was such inhuman, unimaginable misery, such a terrible disaster . . . it would not fit within the bounds of consciousness. I fell ill. For an entire year I could not write."

Starving, bloated bodies lay where they fell—the children, the animals—it was unspeakable. Millions died, but not Rivka and her family. Of course, they couldn't emigrate. No one was allowed out by then. But they survived, as they would survive Stalin's purges of the thirties. No neighbor denounced them as traitors, the midnight knock on the door never came. How did they get so lucky?

• • •

In the early thirties, the Vaks moved from Mogilev to the town of Uman, not too far from Kiev. A year or two later, Betya was sent to study at a teacher training school in Odessa. She spent a year in Odessa and then decided to study music at the conservatory in Kiev. I have her school report, dated 1939. Her photograph is pasted on the cover: at nineteen, her face is rounded with baby fat, like her mother's at that age. She wears her dark hair in a coronet of braids. Her school report describes her as a satisfactory student, passable at languages, good at music. Her instrument was the harp. A famous Russian harpist heard Betya play in Kiev and took her to the conservatory in Moscow for further study. Her brother, Yefim, visited her in Moscow, heard her play in concert, and wrote a poem to her:

> The pen is trembling in my hand . . . you my sweet sister
> you play on the harp with the souls of your fingers
> music has risen to the heavens
> Oh how envious I am of you that the sounds of the strings
>   obey you
> I would give up everything if this favor from god would be
>   given to me . . .

That sort of thing. Sweet, full of genuine feeling if not literary promise. But by that time Yefim wouldn't have had much competition in the literary field. Mandelstam, Babel, Meyerhold, Pilnyak, more than a thousand of Russia's glorious artists, had been arrested and executed. On the night of May 29, 1939, Isaac Babel was interrogated:

*"You have been arrested for treacherous anti-Soviet
activities. Do you acknowledge your guilt?"*

"No, I do not . . ."

"Do not wait until we force you! Begin your confession."

Yefim titled the poem he wrote to his sister "Golden
Sound" and dated it May 1, 1941. Betya's school year had two
more months to run. After that, she planned to spend an indolent
summer with her parents in Uman. It was true that Europe was
at war, that Hitler had marched into Poland, Belgium, and
France. But Russians had nothing to fear. Hadn't Stalin signed a
pact with Hitler? He had shown his good faith by sharing with
Hitler his information on the Polish resistance, so that Hitler
might more easily destroy it. In the name of Nazi-Soviet friendship, Stalin had gone further: he had rounded up, and returned
to Hitler, the thousands of German Communists who had taken
refuge in the Soviet Union. And yet, on June 22, a bare seven
weeks after Yefim wrote his poem, the German army overran the
Ukraine, and Rivka found it necessary to warn Betya: *Do not
come! It's dangerous.*

Mogilev, Murafa, Uman, it made no difference. Almost every
Jew in those towns was either murdered on the spot or marched
to concentration areas to be killed. The Germans came for the
Jews of Uman on September 16. The men were taken away first,
ordered to dig long ditches in front of the airport. Aron was
taken with them. Rivka ran through the streets, screaming in
terror. She wasn't the only woman screaming.

Guards—Germans and their willing helpers, Ukrainians—

were stationed at the airport square and the railroad station to prevent escapes. An order was posted on the streets of Uman: all Jews, of all ages, were to assemble the following morning at the airport to register for a census. Those who failed to appear would be severely punished.

Tables were set up in the square. Jews lined up. But no count was taken. Instead, they were ordered to undress and hand over everything they carried. Clothes and jewelry were placed on the tables. Men and women, mothers carrying babies, stood naked in the dawn light. In front of them were the ditches. Then the screams began again as one line after another was mowed down with automatic pistols. A German lieutenant named Erwin Bingle, stationed in Uman that day, has left us his recollections of this event:

> *Nor were the mothers spared the terrible sight of their children being gripped by their little legs and put to death with one stroke of the pistol butt, or club, thereafter to be thrown on the heap of human bodies in the ditch, some of which were not quite dead . . . The people in the first row thus having been killed in the most inhuman manner, those in the second row were ordered to step forward. The men in this row were . . . handed shovels with which to heap chloride of lime upon the still partly moving bodies . . .*

Even considering that the work had started at dawn, the numbers are staggering: in only one day, and without special killing equipment, twenty-four thousand Jews were gunned down in Uman on September 16, 1941.

· · ·

Betya did not set foot in Uman until the seventies. She found, to her surprise, that her parents' house was still standing. She knocked on the door. A woman answered.

"Did you know my parents?" Betya asked.

"Oh yes," the woman said. "I knew them when I was a child. I was in the grave. I was saved at the last moment. I saw your mother in there."

Betya was in Moscow through the war years. Yefim went into the army. He was a dreamy, artistic boy, but he fought and survived a number of battles. In 1944 he was fighting in the Crimea; on April 28 he was killed in a battle near Sevastopol.

The Germans were on a direct path to Moscow. On September 19 they occupied Kiev; two weeks later, they drove the Jews of Kiev into a deep natural ravine in the forest at Babi Yar and slaughtered them as they lay. As the Germans moved closer to Moscow, Stalin evacuated the government from the city, though he remained. By late November, two German units were in the Moscow suburbs, within sight of the Kremlin. Imagine the fear and chaos: the government gone from the city; factories, offices, and schools shut down; heating, sanitation, food supplies, the infrastructure of civilized life—all on the verge of collapse, and the Germans in sight. But on November 7, Stalin staged the traditional military parade in Red Square to honor the anniversary of the revolution. Some spectators might have regretted the absence, in this time of war, of the best and finest officers of the Red Army and Navy. Stalin had purged—shot—more than fifty thousand of them between 1937 and 1939. Nevertheless, the spectacle had its intended effect. Moscow rallied. The remainder

of the army mobilized. Citizen volunteer divisions were organized. Women served as nurses for the wounded, and as snipers.
The Russian winter froze the German army, along with their
tanks and equipment, but the bombs kept falling. The Battle of
Moscow cost tens of thousands of lives.

What happened to Betya during the war? At the very least,
Red Cross documents show that between June 1941 and August
of the following year, she gave over five liters of her blood. And
yet, miraculously, in 1942, although there was little food in the
city and no way to keep warm, the music conservatory reopened,
and Betya was lucky enough to get a job playing with the orches-
tra at the Central Children's Theatre.

And there is another photograph: pretty, dark-eyed Betya
stands between two handsome soldiers. She looks happy. She is
in love. On the back of the photo, the soldier she loves has written, TO MY BELOVED BETYA. The date is January 1942. The
soldier's name is Isaac Gershlibersohn. He was born in Kharkov,
had moved to Moscow to study acting, and when war came, he
joined the Red Army. Eventually he was sent to the western
front, where he was killed, fighting in Poland, in October 1944.

It seems to me that I recently read something about that
period of the war. October 1944? Yes. The Warsaw Uprising
had begun in July of that year. The Polish Home Army was desperately fighting the Germans, certain that Allied help would
soon arrive. By mid-September, the Red Army had reached the
eastern bank of the Vistula. The Poles could see them. Help was
in sight. But the Red Army stopped at the river's bank and
camped there, under Stalin's orders, for two months, as the Germans destroyed the Home Army and razed Warsaw. Perhaps this
should not have been a surprise. When, under the terms of his

pact with Hitler, Stalin had occupied eastern Poland in 1939, he had murdered thousands of Polish officers in the Katyn forest. Now, close to the war's end, he wanted no resistance to his plans to take over all of Poland as a Soviet satellite. When the Red Army finally moved into the city in October, all was quiet, except perhaps for a few remaining German snipers, one of whom may have taken a shot at Isaac Gershlibersohn.

This is sheer conjecture, except for the fact that Betya lost her sweetheart in Poland in October 1944, and that she gave birth to his daughter, Liya, in war-torn, starving Moscow that same year.

Of course I knew about the war. Didn't we listen to the war news on the radio every night? Didn't I scrape the silver foil from my father's packs of Pall Malls, smooth the foil carefully into sheets, and bring them to school for the war effort? But did I think the war had anything to do with us? Not really. Did I know how frantically my mother and her sisters searched for Rivka and Betya? Honestly, I didn't know these people existed.

In 1947, two long years after the war had ended, Betya managed to get word out. For a brief moment, it seemed that the family in Russia had once again pulled off the trick of survival.

Betya, dearest one born to us,

> *We read in the Jewish paper that you are looking for us. It's hard to describe how we felt when all hope was already lost that any of you stayed alive. Betya dear, you wrote in the paper that because of the war "we lost contact with all our dear ones." Betya, who are the "we" you speak of? Is it possible*

that your parents and brother are still alive? Right away, dear one, send us a letter by airplane, and tell us everything in detail.

We, too, tried very hard to find you. Our cousin wrote from Nikolaev that in Uman they killed everyone. Letters which we sent to Uman came back from organizations that tried to find you.

All of us are waiting to hear from you immediately, to find out about all of you. Grandfather says that you should tell us whatever you need and we will send everything.

This is Frieda. I am writing for everyone, for Rachile, Bella, Leiza, Haskell, Iosif, Berka.

I'm hugging you my dear one.

Soon they knew that only Betya was alive, trying to survive with her child in a devastated city. What I remember of this time, by now the fifties, is orgies of shopping. Daily telephone conversations between one or another or all of the sisters, arranging to meet at Macy's, Klein's, or Orbach's, where they searched for bargains and returned home with huge bundles of clothes that had to be wrapped and shipped to Moscow. Why clothes, not money? Soviet citizens were not allowed to receive money. But clothes, especially warm coats, were currency that Betya could sell or trade.

Betya married. We know that Liya's father died in the war, but the other soldier who appeared in the photograph with them had come back. His name was Alexander Gordeev. He had trained as an actor at the Moscow State Jewish Theater School.

It's odd to think that there was a moment when Jewish culture flourished in Soviet Russia. In the mid-twenties, it seemed that the promise of emancipation would be fulfilled. A theater was established where plays were performed in Yiddish; Jewish poets wrote poems in Yiddish, newspapers and books were published in Yiddish. When the Moscow State Jewish Theater was founded in 1925, many Jewish artists were involved—the painter Marc Chagall, the writer Sholem Aleichem, the poet Peretz Markish, the internationally known actor and director Solomon Mikhoels.

When war came to Soviet Russia, how useful the Jews proved to be. Stalin organized a Jewish Anti-Fascist Committee, with Mikhoels as chairman. From June to December 1943, the committee toured America, Mexico, Canada, and England to spread the word of Nazi atrocities and involve foreign Jews in support of the war. In 1946, Mikhoels was awarded the Stalin Prize for his work during the war.

It all ended soon, and would have ended earlier if not for the war. In 1939 Mikhoels was already being set up for arrest. The interrogation of Isaac Babel in June 1939 brought forth a denunciation:

> *I met with Solomon Mikhoels, the head of the Jewish State Theatre. With reason, he considered himself an outstanding actor and was constantly dissatisfied [with] the Soviet repertoire . . . He was extremely disapproving of the plays of Soviet dramatists . . .*

Four months later, Babel realized that nothing he said would save him. He took back his forced accusations:

*I slandered certain people and gave false testimony about my
terrorist activities . . . I fabricated my testimony about S. M.
Eisenstein and S. M. Mikhoels.*

Mikhoels was killed in 1948, surviving Babel by eight
years. In 1947, *Pravda* had begun a campaign against "rootless
cosmopolitans," "persons without identity," "passportless wan-
derers." No one doubted which people were meant by these
scarcely disguised euphemisms. Editorials in *Pravda* denounced
Jews as saboteurs of Russian culture, Zionists without loyalty to
the Motherland. Another round of show trials was about to
begin, this one aimed at Jews. In the five years before his death
in 1953, Stalin had ordered the arrest, interrogation, imprison-
ment, and death of Jewish intellectuals, artists, scientists, and
doctors. First they were put on trial. Presiding officer to defendant Solomon Lozovsky:

*What kind of Bolshevik are you, if you believe that Jews
in our country, in the USSR, do not have equal rights? That is
slander.*

Jewish theaters and schools were closed, Jewish newspapers were banned, Jews lost their jobs, Alexander Gordeev lost
his job. Betya's life as a professional musician was finished.
Gordeev eventually found work at a government agency as a
photographer. Betya found piecework with a factory that manu-
factured theatrical props. She worked at home all day, and
sometimes all night, gluing envelopes together, making artificial
flowers, decorating plastic boxes, making braid for the hats of
army officers. She lived off of that and the bundles of coats, and

later the cash, that kept coming from America. As for us, our house filled up with artificial flowers and decorative plastic boxes.

In the meantime, Liya grew up and went to school—to music school for several years, then to a regular school. If she was a strange child, anxiety-ridden, fearful, obsessive, clinging to her mother, the circumstances of her life would have been enough to explain it. But Betya had her own idiosyncracies. She was a woman who took up a lot of psychic space. She was demanding, impatient with Liya, annoyed with her, angry much of the time. Her own life was hard enough. Why couldn't the child keep a job? Why couldn't she concentrate on anything? Why would Liya never leave her be? For a while Liya worked at the Lenin Library, but then she quit or was fired and went from one job to another. She was intelligent, quick-witted, there was no doubt about that. But she was lost. Finally, she stopped working altogether. If there was ever a boyfriend or lover, it came to nothing.

In 1966, Betya and Gordeev divorced, but the family continued to live together in a one-room apartment. There was nowhere else to go. In time, Betya's aunts raised enough money for her to buy a place of her own. She found an apartment in an outer ring of Moscow and moved in with Liya. This is the apartment that Liya cannot bring herself to clean, where the kitchen wall is cracked, where roaches scuttle, where my cousin, now in her early sixties, has lived alone for the last twenty years.

At last I've reached Moscow. Here is my cousin Liya opening the door to the apartment. I see a small, thin woman with a mass of long, curling gray hair. She is smiling; four missing front teeth don't stop her from smiling. She is talking, she cannot stop talking. In her excitement and happiness, she cannot keep still. She sits, she stands, she wants to know everything. She pulls me to the kitchen to make tea. The apartment is as I knew it would be, bare, dusty, a broken bed propped against a bedroom wall, the crack in the kitchen wall, and there they still are, the scuttling cockroaches. We talk. We go to a nearby café; she hungrily eats a plate of fatty pork that I cannot bear to touch, and we wrap up my portion to take home for her dinner. We pass an old beggar woman, and Liya gives her a coin. Back in the apartment, we drink more tea. She opens a bureau drawer and takes out heaps of yellowing photographs, brittle papers, books. She piles them in my lap. I look at the books. I am astonished. *My* books. I look at the photographs. *My* life: a baby in my mother's arms, a little girl holding my father's hand, an adolescent with my cousins, my darling aunts and uncles, my clean, comfortable house, my sweet mother, my wedding day, my full life. What did Liya think as year after year her cousin's life was placed before her? Did she see what I see now? Did she see my great, good, pure dumb luck? Did she see that my road had always been clear and open before me? Why didn't *I* know that?

Acknowledgments

My thanks to Alex Dunai, and exemplary historian and guide to Ukraine, and to Daniel Mendelsohn, who put me in touch with him. Alya Kashper responded to alarms about the well-being of my cousin, Liya Alexandrovna, in Moscow, and also served as my translator in that city. I couldn't have wished for a more congenial traveling companion than my cousin Vivian Mazur.

I am indebted to many scholars of Soviet and Ukranian history: Robert Conquest, Orlando Figes, Anna Reid, and Vitaly Shentalinsky, to name just a few.

Our household wouldn't function without the help of Gilda Caverte and Avelino Caverte, and I thank them from my heart. Now, and always, I am deeply grateful to my first readers, my husband, Ben Sonnenberg, and our friend Michael Train. My friend and editor, Daniel Menaker, is the best of his kind, in both departments.

PHOTO CREDITS

*Photograph of Sigmund Freud's couch on page 2 is
     courtesy of the Freud Museum, London.*

Photograph on page 46 is by Chester Higgins Jr./The New York Times.

Photographs on pages 92 and 102 are © 2006 by Sylvia Plachy.

Photographs on pages 18, 70, and 82 are by Dorothy Gallagher.

DOROTHY GALLAGHER was born and raised in New York City. She was a features editor for *Redbook* magazine and then became a free-lance writer. Her work has been published in *The New York Times Magazine, The New York Times Book Review,* and *Grand Street.* Her three previous books are *How I Came into My Inheritance and Other True Stories,* a memoir about growing up as the daughter of Russian-immigrant Jews in Washington Heights; *Hannah's Daughters,* an account of a six-generation matrilineal family; and *All the Right Enemies,* a biography of the Italian-American anarchist Carlo Tresca. She lives in New York with her husband, the writer Ben Sonnenberg.

ABOUT THE TYPE

This book was set in Sabon, a typeface designed by the well-known German typographer Jan Tschichold (1902–74). Sabon's design is based upon the original letter forms of Claude Garamond and was created specifically to be used for three sources: foundry type for hand composition, Linotype, and Monotype. Tschichold named his typeface for the famous Frankfurt typefounder Jacques Sabon, who died in 1580.